In Search of the Heart

In Search of the Heart

Dr. David Allen

A
JANET
THOMA
BOOK

THOMAS NELSON PUBLISHERS
Nashville

Copyright © 1993 by David Allen.

Published in Nashville, Tennessee, by Thomas Nelson, Inc.

Unless otherwise noted, the Bible version used in this publication is THE NEW KING JAMES VERSION OF THE BIBLE. Copyright © 1979, 1980, 1982, Thomas Nelson, Inc., Publishers.

Examples cited in this book are composites of the author's actual cases and experiences. Names and facts have been changed and rearranged to maintain confidentiality.

Library of Congress Cataloging-in-Publication Data

Allen, David.
    In search of the heart / David Allen.
      p.   cm.
    Includes bibliographical references.
    ISBN 0-8407-7730-2
    1. Spiritual life. 2. Allen, David. I. Title.
  BV4501.2.A4235   1993
  248.4—dc20   92–39632
                                        CIP

Printed in the United States of America.
1 2 3 4 5 6 — 96 95 94 93

This book is dedicated
to the memory of my parents,
the late Bessie and Fred Allen,
who taught me much about the heart.

❦ ❧

Contents

Foreword

It is a great joy for me to introduce David Allen's most encouraging book, *In Search of the Heart*. I came to know David during my time on the faculty of Yale Divinity School and found in him a psychiatrist with a great soul. Seldom did I meet someone who not only was a very competent doctor, but also a deeply pastoral person. His openness, his willingness to be vulnerable, and his deep love for God were always visible in the way he talked to people, met his patients, and cared for his students. David really integrated his own personal journey with God in his medical and psychological training.

In Search of the Heart is a book that is clearly the fruit of a life lived in obedience to God and with deep care for people. David understands the complexity of human emotions and also the powerful influence of God's spirit in our everyday lives. I am very impressed with this book because I can feel David's personal heart loving us and desiring to bring us in touch with the all-embracing love of God—not as a preacher, but as an articulate psychiatrist. He tells many stories about the human struggle and human victory, and he is not afraid to share his own joys and pain as he walks with others. I am deeply convinced that this book will offer comfort and consolation to many people. It is a challenging, but most of all a hope-giving, book.

Dr. Henri Nouwen
Author of *The Wounded Healer*

Acknowledgments

I would like to express my special gratitude for all those hurting persons who taught me so much about myself and sent me in search of my heart. These people helped build on the foundation of faith laid by my godly parents and spiritual mentors along the way.

This book would not have been possible without the expert and wise guidance of my editor Janet Thoma and her staff who worked so hard to help me put in writing the feelings and thoughts of my heart. I shall ever be grateful for Janet's patience and encouragement.

Special thanks to Rita Schweitz who helped with the organization and presentation of the work.

Many thanks to Cherry Sharrer whose enthusiasm and constant prodding encouraged me to push on with the project.

Finally, I'd like to thank my wife, Vicki, and my children, Marie and David, whose love and spiritual support made this book a reality even before it was written.

❧ PART ONE ❧

In Search of our Hearts

1

The Journey of Spiritual Discovery

Anita was twenty-nine years old, pleasant, and attractive. Yet in spite of her casual manner, she was dangerously fed up with life. "My life has come to a crossroads. Something has to happen fast or I'm going under," she said as she wiped a tear from the corner of her eye. "I just can't cope with the stress any longer. I wish I could go to sleep and never wake up."

Anita described her husband as cold, distant, and unsupportive. His job was sporadic and he contributed very little to the financial needs of the home. Her wish that she could go away and never come back led to more overt suicidal thoughts.

To make matters worse, one of Anita's children was having trouble in school. With little involvement or encouragement from her husband, Anita had to carry the burden of helping her little daughter cope with her schoolwork. Anita rose early, cooked breakfast, got the kids off to school, then rushed to work. After work the needs of the children and responsibilities of daily living all fell on her.

Not surprisingly, she was terribly fatigued, depressed, and suffering poor health.

Anita is not all that different from the many people I have treated. Neither is she all that different from you and me. I first realized this in 1972 when I was a third-year psychiatric resident at Harvard. I spent part of that time at a drug-treatment clinic in East Boston.

It had always puzzled me that people could destroy their lives by putting chemicals into their bodies. Many of the addicts at the clinic were addicted to heroin and were on methadone (a drug used to block the craving for heroin) maintenance; even then they sometimes shot heroin or abused alcohol.

I found the work exciting but extremely frustrating. Sometimes I would feel good about a particular patient's progress, then in the next week or so that person was on the clinic's doorstep, drunk again or high on drugs or overdosing on methadone.

One client particularly frustrated me. John, by then a thirty-five-year-old man, had begun using marijuana and alcohol at the age of thirteen; then he went on to heroin. His family was poor; his father was an alcoholic who had abused John and his mother.

We worked very intensely with John in individual and group psychotherapy and with his family in family therapy. We even tried an innovative form of therapy in which we asked John to lie in a coffin to make him realize his abuse of heroin and methadone would kill him in a couple of years. Yet nothing changed John's behavior.

Our failure to help John led me to ask myself, *Is a psychiatrist really needed in the treatment of addictions? Is this a good use of my time as a highly trained medical doctor?* John made me realize I didn't know how to apply the traditional models of therapy to people who had given up on life and lived on the streets. I had asked these same questions when I first began my psychiatric residency. Was I going to learn anything that would benefit my people in the Bahamas? I'd even thought of returning to internal medicine, where I would learn more about healing the physical ailments prevalent on my island home. Having been raised by a loving family in the Judeo-Christian tradition, I struggled to integrate psychiatry and my Christian faith. This struggle was extremely difficult and caused me much emotional and intellectual turmoil.

A professor challenged those thoughts. "You're just running from psychiatry, Allen. Instead why not try to be creative *within* the field of psychiatry?" he asked.

When I thought about John, all of these questions resurfaced. He made me feel so inadequate I did not like him—and also hated myself for being so involved with him.

I will never forget what happened one Wednesday afternoon when I was standing outside the clinic, waiting for John. He was supposed to have an appointment, but as usual he wasn't there. Again I felt I had been set up.

Finally I looked down the quiet residential street lined with broken-down buildings and disheveled row houses and saw John coming toward me. His blond, uncombed hair stuck straight up and out around his haggard, dirt-stained face, a rough beard showed around his chin line, and his faded brown shirt was flowing over his torn, ragged jeans. He staggered left and right as he walked; obviously he had been drinking or shooting up.

I was almost revolted by seeing him. In my heart I was saying, *Not again!*

John must have sensed my frustration. He slurred and said words I will never forget as long as I live: "Youuu knowww, Dr. Allennn, you and I are alike. Youuu see . . . I shoot uppp on heroin . . . and youuuu shoot up on ego."

That velvet harpoon hit me in my heart. It made me realize for the first time that, yes, in many ways John and I were alike. We were both human beings. We were both made in the image of God. We both wanted love. We both wanted respect. We both carried pain within us. John was dampening his pain with heroin. Was I soothing mine with ego?

Was I trying to deal with my own hurt by trying to superintend John's life? Living far away from my peaceful island home in the Bahamas, I wanted desperately to succeed as a psychiatrist in this very sterile, academic atmosphere. But the more I tried to be on top of things and the more I tried to help my patients, the more I realized my inadequacy. John had a huge bomb inside him, ready to explode and destroy himself and anyone else within a mile radius. Yet I also had a similar explosive inside myself that might go off sometime and harm me or my family. And I suspect you do too.

As human beings we all have hurts; we all have a sense of inadequacy, and we do different things to counteract that inadequacy: We shoot up on heroin or on ego, the idea that we have some superior knowledge. I realized the pride in my heart was alienating me from my humanness and my natural empathy with John.

In a very deep sense my own heart was hurt. How could I, who had not dealt with my own hurt heart, touch the hurting heart of John? I had to face my own pain in order to understand his.

In Search of the Heart

The famous child psychoanalyst Bruno Bettelheim, who himself had suffered in German concentration camps, lamented that Freud's concept of the psyche—of working with patients to help them get in touch with the inner part of themselves and find meaning in life—had become cold, technological, and distant. Freud, he said, had meant for this work to be sacred. What we need more than ever in working with people who are hurting is a spontaneous sympathy with their unconscious, Bettelheim said.[1]

In working with severely disturbed children he found that an emotional closeness, which resulted from a sympathetic comprehension of the child's soul, was needed. What we need is a feeling response, he said, from one soul to the next.

This struck a chord in my work because I had spent much of my time working with the mentally retarded, the mentally ill, and persons—including addicts like John— whose lives had been devastated by crime, poverty, and drugs. I, too, had come to realize the need for empathic, heart-to-heart connection, not more psychological fads or sophisticated behavioral theories.

What could I say to a retarded child who said to me, "Fix me"? What could I say to a mentally ill person who asked, "Why do I have to suffer so much?" Or to the twelve-year-old daughter whose mother was raped in front of her and who later asked me, "Dr. Allen, will the man come back and kill me and my family?"

Their pain confounded the remedies of my classical training in psychiatry. As a result of their questions and John's velvet harpoon I was catapulted into a search for deeper meaning in my life and a search to find spontaneous, unconscious sympathy with others. This journey led me to face my pain, my inadequacy, my inner helplessness. I call this journey the search for the heart.

The heart is a metaphor for the center of the person, the inner core where all aspects of the person converge—the physical, the emotional, the intellectual, and the spiritual. The heart is the essence of who we really are involving our body, soul, and spirit.

Sure I can make decisions intellectually, but when I think through my heart, I relate my thinking to what is happening in all aspects of my life. In the same way, when I see with my eyes, yes, I see; but when I see with the eyes of my heart, I go beyond physical seeing to real understanding because I am relating what I see to all the other parts of me. Christ warned about those who, "seeing they may not see, and hearing they may not understand."[2]

The heart is the place that is most personal but also most universal since we reach out to others through our hearts. It is the dwelling place of our values, our love, our commitment, our dreams. It is the source of our attitudes, intentions, and behavior. It is the repository of good and evil, love and hate—the place where we touch the divine.

King Solomon was right when he said: "Keep your heart with all diligence, / For out of it spring the issues of life."[3]

Our challenge is to become missionaries to our own hearts. So often we forget the painful feelings buried deep inside us—anger, fear, guilt—and the experiences that led us to feel that way. The heart is the repository for those painful feelings, but like a sponge it can only absorb so much emotion. Once it's saturated, there's little room left for love and joy and beauty.

And each of us has only so much psychological energy. If we expend that energy dealing with those buried feelings, we have little or no energy left to express or feel love. Even if beauty is there, we can't see it. Even if we are loved, we can't feel it.

John Bowlby found this detachment in the lives of children who were placed in the hospital. When some of their mothers didn't return the children cried and protested for weeks. When their mothers still didn't return, they moved into despair. Finally they cut themselves off from the nurses and doctors and other children in the ward. They became detached. Even if their mothers came back, they would not know them. The children gave their mothers the same smile they gave to strangers.[4]

When our hearts cry out and don't receive what they

need, they finally close, or detach. Then it's hard to feel our own pain and we don't feel others' pain either. I've seen parents who were so detached they didn't know their kids were on drugs, even though they lived with them. I call these "dead living people," and I believe there are more of them than there are "*dead* dead people." One political figure told me, "I feel nothing anymore, Doc. I used to care about people. I went into politics so I could help them. Now I don't care. I feel cut off from my own humanity." He had become an automaton from his overwork and hectic lifestyle. His heart had become detached.

Often in therapy patients will say, "No one loves me." That's not so. The truth is, their hearts are so full of hurt they can't feel the love around them. When hurting people have the courage to work through their pain and release the negative feelings imprisoning their hearts, it's like squeezing some of the water out of the sponge; it leaves more space in their hearts for love and joy and beauty.

Once I started the search for my heart I began suggesting that my patients also follow this journey—going beyond recovery to spiritual discovery.

Beyond Recovery to Spiritual Discovery

Anita had severe financial problems, she was not feeling physically well, and like John, she felt life was hopeless and without meaning. Anita and John both needed recovery. When a person like Anita enters my office with signs of clinical depression and emotional instability, certain medical steps must be taken. In Anita's case suicide or homicide was a very real possibility. Chemical imbalances had to be corrected before she would be free to work on her life without endangering herself.

When an injured person is brought into a hospital emergency room, the doctor must first stop the bleeding. Then, after the patient is stabilized, the physician can do a more extensive examination. In the same way, a person with serious emotional wounds must be treated to regain stability first as if he or she had a bleeding heart. Then, after restoring physical, chemical, and emotional balance, work can begin on the process of recovery: This was the situation facing Anita.

Recovery means regaining what you lost during an illness or event and returning to the condition you were in before the pain began. It involves the decision to reveal the secret of your pain and share it with another. Recovery from a wide range of emotional problems, addictions, and family tensions has been the "in" movement during the past decade. Thousands of people like Anita have sought counseling and support through recovery groups for any number of addictions and problems. As a result, you feel better about yourself and receive inner strength to forsake the destructive behavior or symptom, and move to abstinence. Recovery helps us regain the ability to function in the various roles and situations we encounter in life.

Anita's recovery began with supportive therapy to help her through the tension in her marriage, the frustration in her parenting, and the immediate crisis of her suicidal depression. At the same time, an associate who specializes in child psychology started working with Anita's daughter, sharing the load Anita had been shouldering. After several sessions Anita's belief in herself became stronger and she was mobilized to bring about constructive change. As soon as Anita's life had stabilized, she wanted to talk about some past hurts that were still upsetting her, including one particularly traumatic experience.

Early in their marriage her husband had been involved in an affair; this led to a confrontation between Anita and her husband's mistress. Anita's moral convictions and trust had been deeply violated by her husband's betrayal. Even though ten years had passed, the hurt feelings from that experience were still bottled up in Anita's heart—buried alive there. She had many unanswered questions: *How can I help but be angry at him and hate her? How can I respect myself for staying with him? How can I forgive myself for the laziness in our marriage that may have led him to look elsewhere?*

Eventually Anita was able to get her pent-up rage out in the open. As a result she became more relaxed, her sleeping patterns changed, she became less depressed, and she grew more enthusiastic about her job. Strangely, she also began to feel more positive toward her husband. This was certainly an accomplishment.

At its best, recovery therapy allows you to pick up the broken pieces of your life and break the chains of addiction or destructive patterns of relating. However, if the process of healing stops there, you may be left with a feeling of emptiness; you may be caught up in a vortex of perfectionism, frustration, and isolation. That's what happened to Anita. She said, "I am the emptiest recovering person there is." Or, as a recovering alcoholic told me, "I have given up alcohol and drugs but now I feel empty and meaningless. At least when I used to drink I would go with the boys in the boat and have a good time. I can't take it, Doctor. You have helped me give up alcohol and drugs, but I feel miserable. I am going back to my old life."

I've been saddened by this pattern many times. A distinguished aristocrat who moved in and out of drugs, alcohol, and depression told me, "I have been through recovery over and over again. I know the Twelve Steps backward and forward. But I end up feeling empty. Something is missing."

In 1982, my country, the Bahamas, was overrun by a severe cocaine epidemic. As chairman of the National Drug Council, I worked intimately with hundreds of patients addicted to crack-cocaine. Tough, violent, and fragmented, these young men and women had been blown away by that terrible and powerful drug. Many of them reached a state of recovery, staying off the drug for six to eighteen months. However, even in this state of recovery they had severe cravings and felt isolated; they described a feeling of emptiness, an internal void. But without exception, at least in my program, any person who managed to get through this stage and remain drug-free for two years or more went beyond recovery to spiritual discovery.

Spiritual Discovery

My patients often say to each other, "I'm in discovery. Are you?" They are saying they are in a different stage from when they first recovered from their problems and addictions. In fact, discovery is available to anyone who is searching for a deeper meaning in life—searching for his or her heart.

As I mentioned earlier, I realized my own need for discovery during my early work with addicts and troubled patients. This realization comes to people differently. Sometimes they don't need recovery. Yet they long for a deeper meaning to life. For example, Ted, a bored businessman, came into my office saying, "Look, Doc, I ought to be satisfied with my life. I'm making a lot of money. I've got real estate that provides me with extra income. I have a lot of power. My family's doing well. Yet my life seems to be going nowhere fast. I feel empty." Ted was looking for discovery.

My work indicates that discovery involves moving *beyond* recovery. It involves breaking apart the hardened shell of repressed hurt, unraveling the false coverings woven around the heart for self-protection, and exposing the pearl beneath. As we face our woundedness and admit our brokenness we find something beyond personality and damaged memories. We find a living spirit with a unique identity and a great capacity to love and feel loved because we are made in the image of God.

The word *discovery* comes from the Latin prefix *dis*, which means "to break asunder," and the Latin word *cooperire*, which means "to cover, to conceal." Thus, discovery is breaking apart the false covering so the real self—the heart—though hurt and wounded, can rest complete in God's love. There is a space for God in all of us. Some call this the search for fulfillment, the desire for love, or the longing for inner peace. As Saint Augustine said, "Thou hast made us for Thyself, and we shall ever restless be until we find our rest in Thee."[5]

Spiritual discovery anchors a person in the reality of love and peace, faith and trust.

How About You?

You might be wondering, *Where am I in this process?* I often ask my patients to check the statements below that apply to them as they consider this question.

☐ I sometimes fear becoming intimate with someone because he or she might abandon me.

☐ I don't like to be alone. I'd rather be with other people who affirm me.

☐ I tend to overreact to events.

☐ I try to please others, which may be my way of establishing my meaning and identity.

☐ I love my spouse or friend and at the same time tend to hate him or her. (Psychiatrists call this "close ambivalent attitudes," desiring and rejecting someone at the same time.)

☐ I am tired and fed up most of the time.

☐ I sometimes feel very depressed.

☐ I'm often afraid to trust someone.
☐ I have no meaning in life.
☐ I sometimes back away from a relationship because I feel the other person might try to control me. (We call this "engulfment.")
☐ I need a drink at night to relax.
☐ I use food to make me feel better.
☐ I use drugs when I am depressed.
☐ I blame myself for a lot of the problems in our family.
☐ My life seems empty and boring.
☐ I often don't have much motivation to do anything.
☐ I feel empty inside.

If you checked one or more of these statements, you may be searching for discovery, a deeper meaning in life.

The Process of Discovery

Discovery is no quick fix. It is a process that occurs over time, sometimes ranging from months to years. It is not some advanced super-spiritual state that leads to a superior and escapist attitude on life. Neither is it a scientific formula that can be applied to all persons in all situations. Discovery develops uniquely for each of us because we are dealing with our inner selves. Discovery may occur as you appreciate the peaceful ebb and flow of the ocean highlighted by the soft glow of a setting sun or as you listen to a sermon in church. It may occur at the end of psychotherapy or after some tragic experience that forces you to reexamine your life. The common denominator is a deep sense of love, peace, and joy that persists despite the pain and doubts of life. Discovery enlightens the eyes of the heart so that we may really know faith, hope, and love.[6]

Discovery involves four stages: awareness, confrontation,

commitment, and vocation. These components may not occur in the sequence described here.

Awareness

Becoming aware of the need for a deeper meaning of life or a deeper walk with God is the most important prerequisite to discovery. It is a state of humility that allows us to face the truth of our hearts regardless how painful. As a hungry and thirsty person searches for food and water so a broken heart sends a person looking for discovery. This explains why the people in recovery who admit their limitations and pain are sometimes more open to seeking a deeper meaning in life than those who deny their problems.

Even when Anita's life was going much more smoothly because of insights she gained during therapy, she still spoke of feeling empty. She had regained control over her destructive lifestyle through therapy, but she was only back to where she started: empty. Her life still lacked a sense of meaning. She began to ask searching questions, which she had to answer for herself:

- *Where is my life headed?*
- *What's the purpose behind all the effort?*
- *Why is love worth it?*

Confrontation

When no longer enslaved by drugs, cravings, and other destructive feelings and impulses, the recovered person stands unfettered at the threshold of choice. This is where I was when I began to feel overcome by the hopelessness of my patients' problems and John threw his velvet harpoon at me.

So far so good. But even with the right psychological outfit, or raw material, there still remains the issue of making the moral decision. We may be like a child who clearly understands a rule and is fully capable of doing the right thing—and chooses not to.

We are in a position similar to the slave in ancient times who was chained to a stake. He walked monotonously around the stake, longing to be free. His only escape from the pain of his condition was to dream of freedom, seeing himself roaming the distant, rolling, verdant fields. In his mind he was growing corn in that lush soil and living with a wife in his own home.

According to the legend an angel came as the slave slept and broke the chain. When the slave awoke and saw that the chain was broken he jumped up and headed for the distant hills. Suddenly his heart filled with fear as he thought about the dangers lurking in those unknown regions. *There may be lions out there or hostile warriors who do not like me and try to hurt me. Or I might get lost. On top of that, I have never farmed before. How would I begin?*

Terrified by the prospects of the unknown, the slave walked back down the hill, grabbed the familiar-though-broken chain, and began to walk around the stake as before. As he trudged around and around in that perpetual circle he rationalized, *This is where I've been. I know what to expect here. Maybe it's not so bad after all.*

Human beings can adapt to pain as well as joy; pain can become a companion. A slave mentality will always choose bondage, even though freedom is available. Often the bondage in our own hearts enslaves us more than external restraints. Conversely, if the heart is free and unfettered, then even when we are physically imprisoned we are freer than our captors. In a Nazi prison camp, author Victor Frankl found far more inner freedom than his prison guards.[7]

The ultimate goal, then, is not merely to recover one's

capacity for healthy choice free from destructive influence or to find normal life abhorrent. The goal is to step across the threshold of choice, deciding to take the first steps on a journey to enter fully into life.

As Anita went beyond recovery into spiritual discovery, she gave up her pain—first in therapy with me. And then in prayer to God, the ultimate Healer. Discovery: This is the step of commitment.

Commitment

As Anita worked through her trail of hurts, she wanted to know my thoughts about prayer. She asked me about my personal beliefs: "How does your belief in God give you the strength to keep reaching out to others like me and sharing our pain?"

It can be dangerous for a patient to copy a therapist's method of relating to God because that relationship is personal so I told Anita, "My approach is not necessarily yours. Anita prays as Anita. David prays as David. There can be no formula; my approach can only be a guide." I encouraged Anita to make her own spiritual journey.

One Sunday I was teaching an adult class at my church and I looked around to see Anita sitting in the back of the room. At our next therapy session I said, "Didn't I see you in my Sunday school class last week?"

"Yes," she said. "I've worked through a lot of my hurt with you, and I've told you a lot about it. Now I find myself wanting to deal with some things I can't even tell you. Although I've told you a lot, I still feel there's so much more in me."

Anita looked directly at me. "I've started to pray. I want to talk to God about these things. So when I heard that you teach a Sunday school class, I decided to attend. I came to see exactly what you were saying about the spiritual life."

At that moment Anita went beyond her commitment to

express her feelings to me and began openly committing herself to God. Inside herself she was saying, *Yes, I have pain in my life. I have worked through some of those feelings. But there's some stuff I really can't get at. So, Lord, I'm opening my heart now to ask You to hold me, to guide me, to help me.* She surrendered herself and her hurt—her heart—to God. But she couldn't do that until she had confronted her feelings—some of them in recovery, even more in discovery.

There is a level to human pain that I call the silent level. The deep pain. The inexpressible feelings. No matter how hard we try individually to heal this pain and no matter how good the therapist is, we still need the help of God. The surgeon may cut. The physician may prescribe. The psychiatrist may listen. But only God's love can heal. We doctors can be vehicles of healing if we are humble enough to allow God's love, the healing force of the universe, to move through us to touch our patients.

Spiritual discovery is the process of continually yielding to God the wounded self—the heart—for growth and development. This is a complete revolution (a "metanoia") in which we move away from our egocentricity, or selfish heart, to be open to God's love. As growth continues, the repressed material moving from our unconscious is given over to God. The result is a renewal in the spirit—the creation of a new heart—or what I call the development of the mature self.

Eventually Anita began attending a women's fellowship with a friend and found it extremely supportive. One day she came into the clinic and announced, "I have a new outlook on life."

I asked her what that meant.

"I have made a decision to submit myself completely to God's love and I have received His forgiveness," she said. "I have made Jesus Christ my higher power. This has given me a renewed sense of hope in my life and a deeper compassion for others."

Anita had become a missionary to her own life. Was her spiritual life real or only another passing mechanism to cope with her heartache? In the following weeks I watched for outward signs of inner change, and I was struck most by her new sense of community with those in her small prayer group and by the sense of hope that replaced her familiar litany of "the things that are wrong with my life today."

Vocation

Finally, this intimacy with God erupts in a renewed sense of vocation, which is expressed in the development of a new relationship with ourselves and with others. I believe the Christ wants us to relate to each other as He related to His disciples during the Last Supper—with love, with communion, with commitment despite resistance, with humility, with simplicity, with willingness to serve and be served, and within a transcendent perspective. These seven attitudes of the heart are described in the last seven chapters of this book.

They are not a panacea. They are simply a guide that I have found helpful in my own search for a deeper meaning for my life. They also have helped in my work with patients who wish to leave shallow, superficial living to enter the spiritual depths of our walk with the Holy Other. My hope is that these qualities of the heart will encourage and direct you in your search for authentic identity, intimacy, and meaning in life, just as they did in Anita's life.

As I watched her journey continue, she began to share the principles of the deeper life she now enjoyed with others around her. She discontinued her antidepressant medications, and eventually I was able to terminate therapy.

I was proud of Anita. She had confronted her pain, given up her hurt feelings, and was able to open herself to receive the love of God and of others. She had become a missionary to her own heart. The outflowing of this inner well-being has improved her closeness with her family and increased her love for her friends and community members.

Anita will face new challenges, of course—discovery is a continuing attitude of openness to growth and change throughout our lives. The discovery process is a gentle awakening to abundant life, not a quick fix or dependency upon the advice of a therapist.

If you weed out the negatives in your heart, the positives will have more room to grow; but love does not blossom unattended. You must nurture your ability to see beauty and *express* love, while gently expanding your capacity to appreciate blessings and *receive* love. The way to another's heart is through your own. If your heart is bound up with hurts and bitterness and regrets you cannot reach out fully to others until those destructive emotional chains are broken.

This is an inner and outer journey toward love, and I long for every reader to experience it. The examples and exercises in this book are intended to assist you in this journey, but they are not to be used as tools for manipulating yourself or others into living happily ever after.

My confrontation with John led me to a new enthusiasm for my work and the realization that my faith and my work could be integrated in a dynamic way. All human beings are made in the image of God, with dignity and value. All of us are also flawed. Yet we can struggle to help each other. Even though our problems are different, there is a sense of sameness. We are *all* in need of God's love, protection, and guidance.

In Chapter 2 we will look at the ways past hurts can hold us back in our present lives. To demonstrate the process of healing damaged emotions and moving on, I will share with you the journey I took back into my own childhood experiences.

2

Our Hurt Trail

One sunny Sunday morning when I was eight years old, our minister called to me just as I was leaving church. The short, heavy-set man chatted with me for several moments, then said, "You know you're not the *real* David Allen, don't you?"

I looked up at the man who had been our minister for years. He was smiling as if he were joking, and I knew he was a loving person so I trusted him. Yet, I wasn't sure what he meant. I waited for him to continue.

"We buried the real David Allen years ago," he said matter-of-factly. "He was born about two years before you were, but he developed pneumonia and died." His brown eyes were smiling, but what he was saying was no longer a joke to me—nor to my family, I suspected. Our minister went on to say that the funeral was held in my family's living room and he conducted the service.

Shocked and puzzled, I remained there, standing silently for a while, then I ran off to play so I wouldn't have to hear any more.

An hour later I still felt sick and confused so I hurried home to ask my mother about the "other" David Allen. I found her in the kitchen, preparing dinner for our family of seven. I blurted out my question immediately. "Mom, was there another David Allen? A baby who died?" She stopped rinsing the lettuce, shut off the water, and turned to me without saying anything. For a moment she stood looking at me, an unspoken question, *Who told you?* in her eyes. Then she looked down at her hands and said softly, "Yes, there was.

"Your older brother, David, was a very handsome baby with wonderful curly black hair. When he was about nine months old, he got sick; he began vomiting and his fever soared. Within a week he died of pneumonia. He was such a dear little baby. Everyone commented on his black hair and big dark eyes." She talked a little more about this special baby, and I was struck by how much she loved him. Finally she said, "A year after your brother's death you were born, and we gave you the same name." My mother, a short, plump woman with brown hair, turned back toward the sink, switched on the cold water, and began cleaning the lettuce again. Maybe she did so because she was overcome by her sadness. I don't know. I just knew the conversation was over.

Yet I continued to be plagued by questions and jealousy. Did my parents love the first David Allen more than they loved me? Maybe they wished I looked more like him. But my hair was brown and dull, not beautiful and black. And Mom talked about how good the baby was. I knew there were quite a few times Mom didn't think I was so good.

I remember feeling strange and unsettled. What did it all mean? Who *was* the real David Allen? Now, as an adult, I still look back on that experience with some confusion. Was I conceived to heal my parents' grief? That's a heavy burden for a kid to start off with! And I wonder if my mother worried every time I had a little cough as a child, thinking, *Is he going to die too?* Did she see me or baby David at those moments?

When I look at photographs of myself as a child, I am struck by how serious I was, even at the age of two. Did I somehow sense that I had been born to heal my parents' grief? That minister's jarring words forced me to consider the universal question, _Who am I?_ at an early age. Am I the healer of my parents' grief or am I a person in my own right? Is this the reason for my desire to please, to make everything look good, to make everyone feel better? I believe that bringing people out of sorrow is a storyline written deep within the script of my life.

Although your early childhood memories may be less unsettling than mine, you also experienced events that shaped your life. In general, a person's physical or chronological growth occurs automatically when he or she receives air, water, food, and light.

Not so with our emotional and spiritual growth. As we develop we endure numerous hurts and abuses that form a continuum from minor embarrassments to major emotional trauma. This is what I call the "hurt trail." Each life also contains a string of affirming, inspiring experiences that I call the "love story" (we will talk more about that in Chapter 5). A child is particularly vulnerable to the lasting effects of painful experiences because without help he or she lacks the coping mechanisms to process intense emotion. Children may have very good parents who simply fail to realize how significant something is in their children's view, as my parents sometimes did.

In contrast, most adults seem to have the skills necessary to come to terms with their hurt trails.

The Hurt Trail

The second major event of my own hurt trail centered on a school track competition. In the Bahamas, each school has an annual sports day. The winners from each school compete at an all-city meet.

I was determined that I was going to be the champion of my age group, the nine-year-olds, in the hundred-yard sack race. I exercised and practiced hard every day after school. I put myself on a training diet. I took vitamins. I ate spinach. I even took cod liver oil tablets. When the day came, I won easily and was automatically selected to represent our school in the hundred-yard sack race at the city competition. It was a great honor to compete in the all-city meet; it would be an even greater honor to win.

So I began to train all the harder for the big race. I didn't know it at the time but this race represented a passage in my emotional development. Between the ages of six and eleven a child sees industry—winning and achieving—as a way of overcoming the natural inferiority he or she feels. I unconsciously thought my winning the sack race would establish my worth. Thus, the race was more than just a physical contest; it was an emotional duel to establish who I was in the world. I might not have been able to tell you that at the time, but I did know this race was very important to me.

I went to bed early the night before the race and was up at the crack of dawn. My mother had made a special uniform for me in our school colors: white cotton shorts with a yellow stripe, a white shirt, and a matching yellow cap with a white stripe.

My dad drove me to the big meet in his green Chevy pickup. I was so excited I immediately ran onto the track. The referee came over right away and told me to leave. "It's not time for your race yet," he said. "Pay attention to the program, son. It'll be another hour."

I moved to the sidelines, my gray burlap potato sack in my hands. An hour later that same referee finally announced the hundred-yard sack race, *my* race. I ran to the starting line and eventually heard the words, "On your mark, get set . . ."

The gun went off. I shot off the starting line like a coiled spring. A couple minutes later I looked to my left and right. No one was beside me. I quickly glanced back. The other boys were several yards behind. My dream was coming true! I ran confidently to the finish line.

Once there I jumped out of my bag and waved the gray sack high in the air in the universal sign of victory, thrilled to be the champion.

But no one was clapping! In fact, a great silence fell over the track. Everyone in the stands seemed shocked.

The referee rushed up to me. "Allen," he yelled, "you're disqualified. You jumped out of the sack before you crossed the finish line." He signaled for me to get off the track.

As I walked away I could see the boys who were behind me cross the finish line.

I felt a pain in my chest. I tried to swallow, hoping it would go away. I wanted to burrow deep into the ground. In that moment all the months of training and all the excitement of the night before went through my mind. I could feel the eyes of the crowd on me. Then, to add insult to injury, one of my closest friends came up to me and said, "David, that was a stupid thing to do! You were winning the race and you stopped just before the finish line."

I felt embarrassed, ashamed, and scared.

Not too long afterward my father took me home in our pickup truck. He didn't have much to say, and I couldn't figure out if he was quiet because he was also embarrassed or if my losing just didn't matter that much to him.

When I entered our house, Mom asked, "How did the race go?"

I told her what had happened. "Oh, that's too bad," she said, and then went back to dressing my baby sister.

I went directly to my room. The pain in my chest and the

lump in my throat just wouldn't go away. I kept thinking, *If I could only start this day over . . .* But nothing could change what had happened or take away the ache inside me. My friend was right: It was a stupid thing to do. No one realized how much I hurt for the next week or so. Sometimes our parents just don't see the significance of such events.

Sadly, a child's world is very fragile, and so often when children are hurt their world falls apart. The child looks for support. If that support is not available or accessible, the child buries the hurt deep inside. As this process continues, these hurts, embodying many feelings and psychic energy, are repressed within the inner real self. Then the child develops a defensive, false self to cope with the world.

This false self defends the inner, hurt self from the surrounding world. The child's reasoning goes something like this: *If they want me to smile, I'll give them a smile. If they want me to be good, I'll just swallow my pain and be good.* The child learns, early on, *If I fake it, I'll make it.*

The child uses another maxim to deal with others: *If they will let me keep my hurt self hidden and protected from further hurt, I will do all I can to please them.*

Once, during a therapy session, a mother told me, "He was my perfect child. If I told him to sit he would just sit there and be quiet for hours."

Her son, now an adult, replied, "Little did you know, but I was hurt and scared inside. That's one reason I sat so still. Yet even now I feel that same gut-wrenching fear. I'm still shy and afraid of life."

It amazes me to see to what lengths a child will go to make an adult happy.

Repressed childhood hurts and other hurts later in life unconsciously contaminate our behavior, causing many different problems—anger, codependency, depression, an addiction to food or work or drugs or alcohol.

The apostle Paul wrote, "When I was a child, I spoke as a child. . . . but when I became a man, I put away childish things."[1] Physical growth and development take place automatically, but emotional development requires a choice. And that choice is not so hard when you realize what you don't work out, you will act out.

We tend to let what happened to us in the past define who we are now and what we will become. After the great sack race, I saw myself as a loser, someone who couldn't finish the race. Hurt people let pain give birth to more pain.

Defined by the Past

When we experience continual hurt, a destructive process is established inside us. These destructive tendencies may be acted out against ourselves or against others in several ways, including the following three situations.

1. Hurt people hurt people.

A parallel to this destructive process is seen in a child's development. After birth the infant realizes he and his mother are not one (a process psychologists call "the differentiation phase"). He thought his mother's breast belonged to him and was actually a part of him, so he was puzzled when her breast left his mouth, even though he wanted more milk. Feeling angry and disappointed he felt sorry for himself. He has learned a basic lesson in life: What he thought was his was not.

Not to be outdone, the child seeks to strike back when he is weaned from the breast to the bottle. He cries for his bottle, and his mother quickly brings it. Upon receiving the bottle, the child quiets down, but as soon as his mother leaves the room, he throws the bottle on the floor and starts wailing. Psychologists call this "the masochistic defense" because the child defends against his hurt and helplessness by creating his own pain. It is as if he says, *The first time I cried, I was helpless because somebody else caused my pain. But the second time I cried, I was in control because I caused my own pain.* Similarly, an abused person adopts a masochistic defense and creates his or her own pain.

We also believe that victims recreate their pain because they hope to eventually master it—to somehow set things straight (a process called "repetition compulsion"). I tell my patients, "What you don't work out, you tend to act out. Either you choose to work through your hurt trail or you choose to repeat a similar hurt later in life—on yourself or others."

When Charles was six years old, his father left his mother for another woman, moving out of town and severing all contact with his former wife and son. Charles's mother was hurt and dejected. Charles tried to keep up a good front to hide his pain, but he found it unbearable. On Mondays his schoolmates would brag about what they had done with their dads during the weekend. Sometimes Charles would make up lies to give the impression that he, too, had a dad. Nights were particularly difficult. Then the pain was sometimes so heavy on his chest he would cry himself to sleep.

Charles determined to become a doctor, believing doctors were powerful and could overcome pain. He became a successful physician, married a lovely Christian wife, and had three daughters.

When Charles learned his uncle had died he dreaded going to the funeral because he did not want to see his father after so many years. Nevertheless he decided to attend. Glimpsing his father after the funeral, Charles felt confused and uncertain. He was not sure whether to go up and punch him, or just be civil. To his dismay, his father walked toward him, and as he came near Charles saw that he was crying.

Before Charles could speak, his father said, "Son, I know what it's like to grow up without a dad. My father died when I was six. It was tough not having a dad around. When you turned six, I didn't know how to deal with the pain, so I left you and your mother. I'm sorry I did to you what was done to me. I want to tell you how proud I am of you. In spite of my failure, you became a doctor."

At the end of their conversation, both men were crying. The doctor was amazed to learn that his father acted out his own pain on his son—the victim became the perpetrator as the repetition compulsion was carried out. How tragic that we may act out our pain against our children if we refuse to deal with it.

2. Hurt people feel restless because the pain in their hearts creates an emptiness inside them that makes it difficult just to "be."

Hurt people sometimes feel restless without knowing why; they find it hard just to _be_. They always have to be on the go—accomplishing something to help them feel good about themselves and escape the empty feelings quiet reflection brings. They tend to be human _doings_ rather than human _beings_.

Do you ever find it difficult to be still and quiet with yourself because quiet times bring an uncomfortable restlessness or a persistent ache? If so, you may rush madly about, doing and then undoing. Wounded people spend little time planning their lives, developing relationships, expressing feelings, and reflecting on their lives. Instead they try to fill each moment with activity so they can avoid facing their inner pain. They often have such a sense of extreme self-consciousness they feel they must justify their very existence.

Eventually the explosion of their repressed feelings and the excessive expenditure of energy leads to burnout, depression, and lack of creativity.

We all divide our lives into groups of things we have to do—things that are urgent or not urgent, important or not important. Hurt people tend to see most everything as a crisis; they nearly kill themselves trying to please. Everything is urgent and important. By responding to every situation this way, they eventually burn out; no one can live in chronic crisis.

As a result, they may become so fatigued they can't focus on anything. Then they may change from a crisis orientation to an obsession with trivia, seeking refuge in things that are not important and not urgent—wasting time, gossiping, staying up late, fiddling with details, defending themselves unnecessarily.

In contrast, people who are in discovery focus on planning, relationships, information gathering, reading, and long-term physical and spiritual training. They recognize that they have been called to be missionaries to their own lives: developing relationships, growing in spirituality, keeping their bodies in shape, and developing their talents. By focusing on these activities, they reduce the number of activities that are really crises while recognizing things that are neither urgent nor important.

For example, the phone rings and we rush to get it, only to find that even though we might have wanted to talk to the person, the call was not all that important. The same is true with meetings. There may be a lot of urgent meetings at the office in which nothing really happens. Human doings get caught in the cycle of trying to do everything and please everybody, making things important that are neither important nor urgent.

3. Hurt people reduce the perspectives of their lives to minimize their chances of being hurt.

Using denial and rationalization, hurt people believe they will be safe from hurt in a restricted sphere. They resist even reasonable risks. Often, however, their world explodes when they are hurt within the so-called "safety area." Sonny, for example, was very attached to his mother. When she died, his life was shattered. In response, Sonny restricted the sphere of his life by burying himself in his work. His pain and woundedness were lessened when he married a woman who was like his mother; the marriage brought new hope and meaning to his life. Work and this one relationship were his "safety area." When, after a long illness, his wife died, Sonny went into a severe depression because he felt he had again been abandoned. He restricted the sphere of his activities again; now the "safe area" was only his work. Yet as he became progressively more depressed, his functioning on the job decreased and he was laid off. A year later he died of a heart attack.

Continuing to restrict or make smaller tunnels for their lives, self-sheltering individuals continue to get hurt. Eventually they restrict themselves completely, closing their hearts to all feeling. They are then unable to appreciate the meaning and beauty of life. They project the pathos and hurt within their hearts so all they can see is the ugliness, suffering, and absurdity of life. And since no one can live with ugliness and meaninglessness all the time, they lapse into depression. Long before they die physically, though, they have already died emotionally. In fact, in cases like Sonny's, the heart attack may even be a wish fulfillment. In Freudian terms, *eros* (life force) is destroyed, leaving *thanatos* (death force) triumphant.

All of these responses to pain are destructive. They are time bombs that reside within us, hurting us—and others.

But there is another response: discovery, the decision to face our pain, our hurt trails. Discovery will not occur unless we are willing to move beyond our false selves (the facades we present to others) to confront the pathos of our inner wounded selves. We choose to become adults when we choose to work through those hurts to eliminate their influence on our lives. John's velvet harpoon, "Youuuuu and I are alike. Youuuu see, I shoot uppp on heroin, but youuuu shoot up on ego," that day in East Boston sent me on the journey of working through my own hurt trail.

Walking Through Your Hurt Trail

I often ask my patients to confront their pain through the following exercises so they won't repeat it. Since our subjective feelings about our own lives and behavior often make it difficult for us to make accurate evaluations, you might want to have a friend assist you in the discovery process. Or perhaps your pastor, rabbi, priest, or church counselor could offer objective feedback. It is also helpful to note your feelings, insights, and decision points in a spiritual journal. Putting things down on paper clarifies your thoughts and makes it easier to reevaluate them more objectively later. That's why the following exercises have blank spaces for you to write in.

Identifying Your Hurt Trail

Use the space below to list the painful experiences in your life, both past and present—rejections, failures in school (like that hundred-yard sack race), tragic accidents, illness, death, sexual, physical, or emotional abuse.

1. _____

2. _____

3. _____

4. _____

5. _____

6. _____

7. _____

8. _____

Now select the four most difficult experiences and record your age when the experience occurred and the persons involved directly and indirectly.

Experience	*Age*	*Persons Involved*
_____	_____	_____
		_____
_____	_____	_____
		_____
_____	_____	_____
		_____
_____	_____	_____
		_____

Now list these four experiences again and record what you expected from your parent, spouse, sibling, or friend but never received. I filled out this portion of my hurt trail like this:

Hurt	Person	I Expected
Baby David secret	Minister	He should have realized this was a sensitive subject. If he wanted to talk about it, he should have checked with my parents.
	My mom	She was the one who should have told me about the first David. When she did talk to me, I wish she could have been more supportive, told me she loved me, and given me a hug to show me that love. Also talked to me about my feelings: "How did you feel when the minister said that? I'm sure it was hard to hear about Baby David from him."
The great sack race	Referee	He could have taken a moment to show me a little compassion: "I'm sorry, son. You gave it a good try." Instead he was cold and seemed to scold me.
	Friend	I wish he had been more supportive. He told me what I already knew: it was a stupid thing to do.
	My dad	He could have said more about how he felt. As it was I

	couldn't tell if he was let down or just not interested.
My mom	*She could have taken more time to talk to me. "Oh, David, I know how hard you practiced for this. You must be hurt." She could have given me a hug to ease the pain. Instead I felt that the pain in my chest was mine and mine alone. The sack race was an important part of my world.*

Way back there in the Bahamas at age eight, I couldn't understand why the people who loved me couldn't touch the pain I was having. I decided to bury my pain and give the world what it wanted—a happy, good David Allen who didn't care about what had happened. As you consider your own hurt trail you will find, as I did, the wounds from the reactions of adults as well as from the event itself. Acknowledge them all. Take a moment now to consider what you expected when you were hurt:

Hurt	*Person*	*I Expected*
_____	_____	_____
		_____
		_____
		_____
_____	_____	_____
		_____
		_____
		_____

_____ _____   _____
                        _____
                        _____
                        _____
_____ _____   _____
                        _____
                        _____
                        _____
                        _____

_____

You might want to take a few days to complete this exercise so you can ask relatives and others about specific details. You might also want to look back through family albums and other pictures. Then you need to think of the feelings that accompanied these experiences.

Write a series of letters to help you to clarify and release your feelings. (I am indebted to John Bradshaw and Norman Paul for introducing me to the use of letter-writing in psychotherapy.) First, it is helpful to write a letter expressing how you felt at the time of the hurt. If it happened during your childhood, write with your non-dominant hand. This will help you feel as vulnerable as you felt as a child and will free you to remember the incident better. For example, here is my letter from little David to adult David:

Dear Big David,

  It must have been very sad for Mom and Dad to lose baby David, and it makes me feel sad too. But why did they give me his name? Was I born to make Mom and Dad feel better? Did they think of him when they saw me? Who is the real David Allen?

  As I think about it I feel heavy inside and I don't

_know what the feeling is. As a grown person do you
still feel it?_

How will it all work out?

_Love,
David, age eight_

Now write a letter to yourself as you are today from the
child who was hurt long ago:

_____

_____

_____

_____

_____

_____

The next step is to write a letter from the adult you are
now to the person you were when the event occurred. First
take several minutes to imagine yourself stepping into that
memory as a loving adult who is comforting the child the
way you longed for comfort then. As you write your letter,
let your feelings flow naturally. Your words don't have to
make perfect sense to anyone else. You don't need to pretend you have your feelings all figured out. Just aim for
openness and honesty. No more secrets. No more pretending.

Here is my letter from David, the adult, to little David:

Dear eight-year-old David,

_Thinking about this subject makes me feel strange
also. And even though I am older now, I can still iden-_

tify with your feelings. It must have been a real shock for you to hear of your brother's death so abruptly. It would have been nice for you to hear about him from Mom and Dad, but we can't change that.

I guess our birth was to counteract the guilt and grief over the loss of little David. That's a lot to put on a child, as if the mission of our birth was to heal our parents' pain.

Much of my life has been trying to please others. Sometimes this is burdensome and requires much energy and time. I feel a strong sense of inadequacy that forces me to work hard to achieve more. But it never ends. Could it be that I am still trying to meet other people's approval to validate my right to exist in my brother's place? Why did he have to die? Why did I live? This is a vicious cycle. I realize now that the only way to break it is to work through the pain in my heart. And that takes time, perhaps a lifetime.

> *Love,*
> *David, adult*

Now write a letter from yourself today back to the child who was hurt long ago:

_____

_____

_____

_____

_____

_____

I also wrote a letter to little David about that great sack race. This was very touching because even as I was considering the experience again I could almost still feel the pain in my chest.

My letter went something like this:

Dear Little David,

I'm so sorry. I'm so sorry about what happened. It's been years since it happened and I still feel it now. As I recall the memory I still ache for you in my heart. It must have been a terrible experience for you to try so hard to be the best one in the race and yet be disqualified for stopping ten feet short of the finish line. There's nothing I could say to make it feel better, except to let you know that I really do love you. I know the feeling of shame but I want you to know I'm sticking with you.

The good news is that you really tried hard, and many times in life you have to keep on trying. You lost that one, sure, and it was very, very painful. But don't let this pain keep you from winning the races you deserve to win. One thing you've learned from this hard experience is that these things do happen in life but we can't just go and hide away. Hang in there. You can cope this time; you can hope for next time. I love you no matter what.

> *Love,*
> *David, adult*

Then I wrote letters to my mother and father and shared with them how I wished they could have understood what I was going through. I acknowledged that they had seven kids and maybe they didn't have time. I explained that I didn't feel they appreciated how very painful it was to train so hard and want something so badly, then fail that way. I wrote this about my hurt feelings: "I know it's my fault. I know I did something foolish. But I wish you could have comforted me or talked with me more. I wish you could have held me or done something. But you didn't seem to reach out to me at a time when I really needed you."

No one needs to see the letters unless you want to share them. The intent is not to blame others or to find excuses for our failures. Later, my parents and I were able to have a heart-to-heart talk about the effect of my brother's death on my life. That is not always the case. Be careful. It is not healthy to open yourself to further abuse if that is the pattern in your family. Neither is it healthy to tactlessly dump your feelings in an effort to manipulate a response from them or to retaliate for the hurt they may have caused you. That is not the way of love.

Finally I yielded myself to God and said, "Hold me, Lord, and let Your love come into my heart. Take away any bitterness and remorse. I bring to You this experience that was very painful in my life. And I leave it with You. I give it up so I can be filled with Your love and healing power."

Tears came to my eyes as I relived the anguish and hopelessness I felt when I made a fool of myself by stopping short in the race. Yet it was a tremendous relief to deal with that because it freed me from the pain.

You may be wondering, *Why is it worth it to go back through all the hurt?* I can answer that by sharing my own experience. Even though the memory of the sack race still comes back to me, it does not have the same effect on me now. The emotions have already been expressed. The "live" experience that remained in my memory so long is finally dead; what is left now is like an empty shell—devoid of feelings. I can still recall the great sack race, but the emotions that were trapped with that memory have finally been released and drained out. I have been freed from the event's destructive power.

Thus the important thing about our past is not what happened, but what we have done with what happened. This process of working through our hurt trail allows us to gain a sense of closure on the past and get on with our lives.

Critics of personal counseling point out an improper emphasis of the recovery movement: the tendency of some individuals to wallow in the past or become obsessively introspective. Yes, that is a legitimate danger. Just as you can hide behind the tree to avoid seeing the forest you can also hide behind the past to avoid seeing how to improve upon it today. (We can also forget the _good_ times as we work through our hurt trails. I always have my patients consider their love stories too. We will look at those memories in Chapter 5.)

It _is_ possible to get overly analytical in this whole process of self-understanding. That's like the joke I heard about the two psychiatrists who were walking down the street. A man passed them on the sidewalk, smiled, and said "Good day." One therapist turned to the other and said, "I wonder what he means by that."

On the other hand, it is also possible to take our psychological state too lightly. _Please seek out competent medical help before you proceed in this book if you have had at least five of the following symptoms within a two-week period:_

- ☐ A depressed or irritable mood most of the day, nearly every day
- ☐ A diminished interest or pleasure in activities, including apathy toward previously interesting work or pursuits
- ☐ Significant weight loss or weight gain when not dieting or attempting to gain weight
- ☐ Sleep disturbances, either too much or too little (Waking at 3:00 or 4:00 A.M. and not being able to fall

back asleep is one of the most prominent indicators of clinical depression.)

☐ Slowed muscle coordination or feeling restless or fidgety

☐ Fatigue or loss of energy nearly every day, not directly connected to exertion or to normal reactions to the death of a loved one

☐ Preoccupation with feelings of worthlessness or guilt

☐ Indecisiveness or diminished ability to think or concentrate

☐ Recurrent thoughts of death (This is often couched in phrases such as, "I wish I could go to sleep and never wake up" or "I wish I could go away and never come back" or "I wish I could end it all.")[2]

The final event I want to share from my hurt trail happened when I was about sixteen years old. School was always very hard for me. I was slow to pick up facts and figures so I had to work very hard. I even had to repeat the eleventh grade because I didn't do well enough. It was hard for me to go back to school that year, knowing my friends had gone on to the higher grade and I was with the kids who had been below me.

The next year, in the twelfth grade, I was at the top of my class. In those days in the Bahamas we took a special exam, the Senior Cambridge Exam, to prepare for university study in England. I wanted to be a doctor so this particular exam was my gateway to life.

The exam was given in November. I remember thinking as I was taking the exam, *I'm not doing as well as I would like;* but when it was finished I thought I had done well enough to scrape by. The exams were sent off to England to be marked and the results came out the following March.

I will never forget the night my father came home and said, "Some of your classmates came into the store today.

They told me you failed your Cambridge exam." My heart
sank. Again I had lost the race. That same old painful hurt
came into my chest along with a hopeless feeling of disappointment that was almost too deep to bear. My career in
medicine seemed to be evaporating in front of my eyes. I
wanted to disappear. I wanted to give up.

I looked at my father as he said, "David, I don't think any
less of you or believe any less in your future." The words
sounded good. Right. But I knew I had let him down. I had
let myself down. What a terrible evening it was.

The very thought of having to repeat a part of the twelfth
grade sickened me, especially after already repeating grade
eleven. The next day while riding to school I saw one of the
teachers. She frowned at me. I felt so small and hurt. I'm
always amazed at how adults can be so cruel to children
when they fail to perform in ways that reflect well on the
adult.

Obviously, this experience was an important part of my
hurt trail. I began to work through it by writing a letter
about this painful memory from David at age sixteen to the
adult David. In my letter I described what a horrible experience it had been and how I never wanted to face anything
like that again. I wrote to my dad, telling him how much it
meant to me for him to say he didn't think any less of me
because of my marks on the test. And I told my mom how I
knew she had felt for me, but how I had longed for her to
hold me or talk about ways to handle the hurt. I felt so
alone in my pain.

I also wrote a letter from David, the adult, to David, age
sixteen. It read, in part:

Dear David,

*What a terrible experience you went through. I can
still feel the pain in my heart, too, because you and I*

are one. No one but you and I know how painful that was. Even today I tighten up when I think about the embarrassment, the shame, the loneliness you went through. The feeling of defeat and humiliation was so awful then; I cry with you. But I also want to let you know that I believe in you. I love you, David. And I want you to realize that you are not alone; you never were, because God loves you too. In fact, as you look back with me now you can see the amazing ways in which God worked. You were able to go back to school, retake the exam the next year, move on to the University of Saint Andrews in Scotland, and graduate in July 1969. Then you completed a general medical internship at Princess Margaret Hospital in Nassau and a three-year psychiatric residency at Harvard to accomplish your goals.

If I could somehow step beside you at that very painful moment in the past I would tell you not to lose heart. Don't give up, David. We're in this together and the successes will be just as real as the failures. This is not the end. Don't give up on your life.

Love,
David, adult

Does this story surprise you, coming from a doctor who has trained and taught at some of the top universities in the world and is the recipient of a number of national awards?

I hope so! I hope you will often be pleasantly reminded that people who *appear* to have succeeded because everything came easily for them may also have faced obstacles and emotional wounds. They, too, have a hurt trail. Stories like mine can give you hope and motivate you. You *can* overcome your past. No one has to have a perfect past to have a good life and a bright future.

The experiences from my hurt trail taught me humility and how to face my shame; those experiences work in a powerful way for good in my life today, giving me new empathy for my children and the hurts they experience. Because I actively accepted and comforted my inner child, I am encouraged to be with my children more, to love them more with my hugs, words, and prayers. I'm sure I'm a much more compassionate father and counselor because of the very things that caused me pain.

As much as it hurt, the truth about the inner void and emptiness inside me was liberating. John did me a great favor that day in East Boston. The discovery process I began then has freed me from self-pity and insecurity. The same thing can happen for you. As you grieve the pain of past traumas and hurts, your feeble, real self can begin to grow. You can come to realize God's love in a special way because He has been there all the time. God is never with the false self; He is always with your heart, the hurting inner part of you.

The good news is that the authentic self, even with its wounds, is still the center of life-changing power. Created in the image of God, each of us has this power to imagine, to create, and to act upon our environment.

As we discover our real selves we can also move beyond our self-centered world to discover beauty, truth, love, and communion with those around us—but not until we have completely dealt with our anger. Each of us has a time bomb within us that will poison our lives if we don't release our anger over these past hurts in constructive ways. That will be our focus in the next chapter.

3

Dealing with Our Inner Anger

Monica was a tall, pretty blonde-haired woman who worked as a professional model. One day she strolled into the reception room of my office, which was located in a nineteenth-century convent started by the Sisters of Charity, and boldly announced, "I want two hours of your time."

Her aggressive tone seemed so incongruous to the peaceful setting of the sunlit waiting room that the two other people in the room looked up from the magazines they were reading and stared at her.

I didn't need to look at my schedule. My day was already overbooked, as Monica should have known when she saw the two patients already waiting. So I told her, "I'm sorry; I have no time available."

"But I want two hours," she replied in a tone that said, *I'm used to getting what I want when I want it.*

"You can't have two hours. But you can have fifteen minutes. It's all the time I have."

"I want two hours," she insisted angrily.

"I can't give you two hours if I only have fifteen minutes," I explained with as much patience as I could muster. I showed Monica into my private office and for the next fifteen minutes she told me a little bit about her life. Then she said, "I need to talk to you for two hours tomorrow."

The next day I waited for her. At 1:15 P.M. there was a heavy knock on my office door, then Monica walked in, drunk. She kicked an antique desk that was very special to me, then shoved it into the wall. A few minutes later she reached over the desktop and brushed the pictures of my wife and children onto the floor.

Again her behavior struck an incongruent note in the small, quiet room. Her anger almost frightened me as she stood straight in front of me and said, "Now you see what I am really like."

"What are you talking about?"

"I'm hurt. I'm hurt. I'm miserable," Monica said.

"Well, I can't work with you—you are drunk." I set up another appointment for the following day.

The next day Monica returned, this time sober, and I listened to her for the full two hours.

"I have a pain I cannot bear," she said as she pushed her long blonde hair back from her face. She stopped a moment and stared intently at me as if trying to decide whether she should trust me. Then she said, "Three years ago my two-year-old child died. I felt guilty because I did not take her to the doctor sooner," she admitted.

I thought of my mother and knew she must have felt some of those same emotions when the other baby David had gotten sick and died.

The pain of her guilt caused Monica's voice to break. Tears began to stream down her face. She bowed her head to regain her composure. Then she looked intently at me again and asked in a loud, vindictive tone, "My baby, how could my baby leave me? How could God do this to me?"

Monica was angry. At God. At herself. Even at her baby for leaving her.

Anger is a temporary emotion we experience when we are threatened physically, emotionally, socially, or intellectually. But when Monica denied her anger and failed to deal with the temporary emotion, her anger became repressed and organized. This repressed anger collected all her other repressed negative feelings and became hate.

Anger is temporary; hate is permanent, fed by our destructive anger. Monica hated herself, her life, and the painful world she lived in. Hate evokes the desire to hurt or wound the hated person. I had seen that kind of hate a few years earlier when I visited prisoners on death row.

I had just returned to the Bahamas and was beginning my psychiatric practice. That cloudy, humid Sunday morning I drove to the prison at nine o'clock to do rounds as "psychiatrist on call." As I neared the prison I saw three armed, khaki-uniformed guards behind the iron gate. They came out when I honked and quickly questioned my reason for being there.

My answer satisfied them, but they still inspected my car. Finally one of the guards got in the car and drove with me to the ugliest, darkest, largest gray building I had ever seen. The guard put a key in the huge metal door and I heard a loud *klung!* as the lock released and the heavy door swung open.

At the end of the dark corridor was yet another gate, this one made of interwoven metal bars. My escort told the guards at this gate who I was and again the gate was unlocked.

At each gate I felt more insecure. What was my role here anyway? What could a psychiatrist do for men who had been condemned to death?

Finally the guard and I walked up a long corridor to the

end, where four cells lined one wall. Finally I saw the men who were locked inside all these gates.

One was big and hefty with tattoos on his huge, muscular biceps. I thought I recognized him but wasn't sure. Another was slight of build. All of them were bare-chested, dressed only in short pants.

The huge man with the tattooed biceps immediately called out to me, "Allen, what are you doing here? What do you have to say to us? We are going to die in two weeks."

I was glad the thick bars were between us. The hopelessness of the caged man and the anger in his eyes scared me. And his insight frightened me even more. He had echoed my own fears.

"Well, I'm not sure what I can say to you," I admitted. "Maybe you have something to say to me."

The two of us stood there without speaking, frozen by the questions between us. Then the slim young man in the next cell said, "Come here, Allen."

I walked toward his cell sheepishly. He told me something I will never forget. He said, "I want you to tell people after I am dead that they better learn how to handle anger." I was surprised by his composure and the confident tone of his voice.

"Let them know, Allen, the same anger they feel every day is the anger that makes us kill each other. One Sunday morning my brother made me angry, and the next thing I knew a jackknife was down his chest and he was dead."

That twenty-year-old man is not the only prisoner who has conveyed to me a chilling warning about the emotion of anger. A few years later I was visiting a teenager who had killed his family. As I was talking with the kid he said, "The old man used to ride me. I just couldn't do well enough in school. Every night he was on me about work, work, work. He always wanted me to perform; he never showed me love, and I just got angry at him. I decided I had to kill him. But at first I was afraid to. So I got his gun, and every day for three weeks I sat in my room with his gun on my knee and prayed to Satan for the courage to kill him."

Three weeks later, he shot his father, mother, brother, and sister.

Anger kills.

All anger. Your anger. My anger.

I've never forgotten the warning of those prisoners. Hurt people hurt people.

The definition of anger is simply "an emotional reaction to hurt." Where there is hurt there is anger; where there is anger there is hurt. The essential issue is not so much the hurt itself, but how we choose to deal with the anger we feel. All anger may be released through destructive or constructive behavior. Anger can motivate positive changes in behavior if we handle it correctly.

Changing the Way We Handle Anger

My wife tells an amusing story that helps demonstrate the need to plan how we will deal with a situation—in this case an emotion like anger. She says she has a friend who is married to a Dutch man and every time her friend's washing machine breaks down, she simply calls her Dutch husband and in a minute it is fixed.

"Well," my wife said, "I can't say the same thing about David. When our washing machine breaks down I call him and he says, 'How do you feel about it?'"

Psychiatrists are good at talking about lovely dynamics, and often we can help you get to your heart, but somewhere down the line, somebody has to fix the washing machine!

I have developed a process to help my patients deal with their anger as effectively as that Dutch husband fixes his wife's washing machine. It involves seven steps:

1. Recognize the problem
2. Assess the effects
3. Take time out
4. Release the anger
5. Transcend the anger
6. Confess the anger
7. Repeat steps 1–6

In the rest of this chapter, we'll see how these seven steps can help you deal with your inner anger.

1. Recognize the Problem

You can't fix anything (even a washing machine) until you understand the deep-seated nature of the problem—in this case, anger—and identify its source. In your emotional life, awareness leads to healing. Many times in therapy a person will say, "I see it. Now what should I do about it?"

I always ask patients to stop a minute and really *feel* the anger gritting inside them. As John Bradshaw advises, "Feel it, name it, claim it, aim it and you will tame it."[1]

Then I tell my patients to begin accepting responsibility for their actions (their response to the anger). At first Monica resisted the idea of personal responsibility. She thought, *I drink because my baby died. I drink to unwind. I'm angry because life is unfair. My little Georgia's early death makes me angry.* It was difficult for her to admit she *chose* to drink. She *chose* to let anger over her baby's death control her life.

Monica needed to accept that she was a person first, with angry feelings. Then she could come to realize that because she was bigger than her anger it did not need to consume her thought life or control her behavior.

2. Assess the Effects

Anger affects us in different ways:

Physically, anger can cause pain such as headaches, abdominal pain, backaches, or stiffness in the neck. The beautiful body that had won Monica many modeling opportunities plagued her with backaches and chronic restlessness.

Socially, anger may lead to race riots, marital disorder, family disintegration, and even outright war. When Monica began smashing pictures and kicking my office furniture it was not the first time she had gone on a rampage.

Emotionally, anger may manifest itself in psychological disturbances such as insomnia, depression, agitation, or paranoid thinking. After her baby's death, Monica became so emotional and unpredictable even her closest friends backed off, suggesting that she seek some professional help.

Monica's wide range of problems fit a common pattern. Let's look more closely at some common manifestations of repressed hostility. Mentally check the following effects of anger that are present in your own life or in your spouse or child.

☐ **Depression**
Depression may result when anger is turned inward. Some psychologists describe depression as "frozen rage." Depression can result from anger at a world gone wrong, anger at the discrepancy between what life is and what we desire it to be, anger at unpreventable loss. Monica drank because she was depressed. When she came to my office the second time purposely drunk she was unconsciously saying, *See! I'm not the nice-looking model you think I am.* She was also saying, *Yesterday you didn't realize my pain. Today it will be so obvious you will do something. What I did to your office today I am also doing to myself.*

Depression also affected Isaac, a tough construction worker who found it difficult to express his feelings. Married for over fifteen years, Isaac and his wife had severe communication problems. Eventually she left the marriage. Isaac became withdrawn, angry, depressed, and suicidal. Drinking alcohol excessively and taking tranquilizers, Isaac recognized he was falling apart, so he finally came to see me and began individual and group therapy.

"I was angry because I was hurting so badly," Isaac said at one of our sessions. "Anger made me mean to others and to myself. Then I got more depressed." As he learned to express his hurt and grief about losing his wife, Isaac was able to cope more effectively with his life.

Mothers of infants and preschoolers often experience periodic bouts of depression. I believe this depression may result from inner anger about the twenty-four-hour-a-day demands of being a wife and mother coupled with feelings of frustration at not being able to handle the children the way they would like. These mothers feel depressed when little appreciation is shown for what they are doing, when they have little time away for refreshment, and when they are given little support and encouragement from family and friends. These mothers need opportunities to honestly express their frustrations without condemnation so their anger won't be bottled up and result in physical illness or depression. And they *must* get the proper rest and relaxation. Ironically, physical illness is often the only way the mother "earns" a break without criticism or guilt.

☐ **Guilt**

Many of us internalize anger by feeling guilty. Some religious persons have overly sensitive consciences and live a guilt-ridden lifestyle. A distorted sense of guilt makes a clear conscience as unlikely as a blizzard in the Bahamas. Because our false selves know much more about our unworthiness and the judgment of God than about God's love for us, we are left facing a powerful, cruel conscience unless we comprehend God's grace and mercy.

Sadly, a rigid conscience without love and trust can make even a religious individual the most miserable person on the face of the earth. This burdens me because I see a lot of religious people, who have been hurt in life, bury their authentic selves and resist opening themselves to the love of God. Religious dogma and traditions of faith cannot heal, but God's forgiveness and unconditional acceptance can.

☐ **Shame**

It is amazing how we can forgive ourselves for failing in some areas of our lives but not in others. For example, it may be acceptable to gossip about a neighbor, cheat in business, be prejudiced, or tell a lie, but mess up with inappropriate sexual actions and we are finished! If we slip in this area, our self-esteem quickly slips to zero.

Sometimes a person thinks, *Well, I've already messed up anyway, so I might as well just finish it.* This person leaves his or her spouse and adopts a wild lifestyle. Often the extreme behavior results from feelings of failure in an area of personal moral codes.

I tell people who have been promiscuous or who have failed in one of these areas, "You may not have realized it but you messed up long before you *thought* you messed up, and God still loves you anyway. All of us have fallen short of God's standard. We all have much to be ashamed of, but because of God's forgiveness we can be restored."

Shame leaves a powerful aftertaste of not being good enough. As a result we may withdraw from close friends, drop out of the church, and break up our marriages. It's as if we must play God and punish ourselves. But the love of the true God extends beyond our own guilt and shame, and brings healing to our life.

Monica was driven by shame. When she was drunk she barhopped to pick up men who would then abuse her sexually. The next morning she was doubly ashamed and felt guilty about what had occurred the night before. That shame drove her to take another drink and perpetuate the vicious cycle.

☐ **Aggression and Violence**

Aggression and violence are powerful and destructive manifestations of anger that can happen to people who are otherwise very calm and may even be religious. In these persons, past hurts buried with the authentic self are encased in explosive anger that periodically seeps out when there is severe sleep deprivation, provocation, or frustration.

Anger can produce rigidity, boredom, and burnout. Repressed angry feelings exhaust our energy, resulting in tiredness, insomnia, irritability, sexual difficulty, and low productivity. This may culminate in verbal abuse or physical aggression, followed in a few days by another outburst to let off steam. But the pressure only builds. Violence breeds violence.

☐ **Passive/Aggressive Behavior**

Passive/aggressive behavior is a subtle manifestation of anger. On the surface the person appears perfectly content and in control, but deep down he or she is angry. This anger seeps out subtly in gossiping, procrastinating, deliberate lateness, or sarcasm. As one wife said, "He's a great preacher, but oh, when he comes home, it's a disaster!"

Let's stop faking. We don't need to *pretend* to be supportive and kind persons; we need to become *genuinely* supportive and kind. Our phoniness destroys other people while leaving us empty and unfulfilled.

Then there is the Gertrude syndrome. Who was Gertrude? A big fat pig I once knew! Gertrude would roll over in the mud, eat her food, vomit it up, eat it again, and continue to roll over and over in the same mud. One day as I watched Gertrude do her thing I realized she represents a lot of us. We just love mulling over and over in our misery, endlessly thinking, *Poor me, poor me.* As one woman full of self-pity whined, "My life is just ordinary. I have an ordinary husband. I have ordinary children. I have an ordinary house. I have an ordinary job."

So do a lot of us!

Another syndrome I often see is the meat-cleaver syndrome. At times we may appear to passively accept a frustration or embarrassment, yet we aggressively berate ourselves on the inside. Just as a meat cleaver cuts up meat, we sometimes cut ourselves up with destructive thoughts and behavior. *I am no good. I am a failure. Nobody likes me. I'll never get this right.* Eventually, these thoughts become self-fulfilling prophecies.

There are much healthier ways to process our anger and frustration. Shame, guilt, violence, depression, or self-pity will not lead to lasting change. As Aristotle commented in the fourth century B.C., "It is easy to fly into a passion— anybody can do that—but to be angry with the right person to the right extent and at the right time and with the right object and in the right way—that is not easy, and it is not everyone who can do it."

As Monica evaluated the effects of repressed anger and pain on her life, she began to see that her depression, guilt, and aggression stemmed from her anger about the death of her baby. She then was willing to admit openly that she felt angry with God, herself, and her little daughter.

3. Take Time Out

It became clear that Monica needed to take time out from her present life long enough to resolve the unfinished business of her past. I ask patients like Monica to complete the following exercises as they resolve their unfinished business.

Check any of the following statements that are true for you.

☐ When I am angry I seldom let anyone see how mad I am; on the outside I try to appear calm.
☐ I often get sick or lose my appetite when I am angry.
☐ I tend to lose my temper and say things I don't mean or things I do mean but could have said in a kinder way.
☐ I become moody or pout when something angers me.
☐ I tend to be patient with *things* but easily angered by *people.*
☐ I tend to be patient with *people* but easily angered by *things* that frustrate me.
☐ I vent my anger differently toward children than adults. For instance:

_____

_____

_____

Now think about a specific event. The first day Monica came into my office she was extremely aggressive. She felt entitled to my time. After all, she was a beautiful model and most men were happy to spend time with her. However, any time someone is that aggressive and angry I know there's another cause for it besides the surface reason.

Anger and hurt always go together. Any time you are angry, ask yourself, *What story is behind my anger?*

Feel the anger and write down some of your thoughts:

When _____

_____

(Record an event when you were angry. Monica wrote, "When my baby died." You might write, "When Jane insulted me," or "When the car broke down," or "When I went off my diet.") I felt angry because *(Monica wrote, "I felt I had killed my baby.")*

_____

_____

What did you do to make yourself feel better? *(Monica wrote, "I drank to make myself forget. I was promiscuous.")*

_____

_____

Looking back, do you consider your response constructive or destructive? *(Monica's answer was obviously "destructive"; yours might be too.)*

_____

_____

Anger results from hurt or frustration. Ask yourself how your anger relates to your hurt trail. Does this anger tie into past abuse, grief, or unresolved hurt feelings?

☐ Yes   ☐ No

If so, what past events are influencing your anger?

_____

_____

_____

Therapy starts to work once patients connect their anger trail to their hurt trail. As Monica told me her story I began to see another person—not the beautiful, hard-shelled

model but the lovely woman on the inside who was so un-
happy. I felt the empathy that is so necessary for a counselor to help a patient.

Monica's false self was melting and her real self was
emerging. Now we could deal with the real issue: her unspoken thought, *I killed my child.*

I could say to her, "OK, let's look at what really happened. Did you really kill your baby, or does the child inside you think you did?"

When something happens to hurt a child, a divorce for
instance, the child often blames himself or herself, believing, *If I'd been a better kid, Dad (or Mom) wouldn't have
left.*

The child buries that hurting experience in his or her
real self and develops a false self. The adult does the same
thing when he or she is hurt because this has become a
natural reaction. Once the adult gets in touch with the
hurt feelings in his or her heart, he or she is free from
shame and guilt.

4. Release the Anger

Some clients feel it helps to express their anger in the
following ways:

☐ Scream in a secluded place
☐ Hit a pillow
☐ Tell off an empty chair
☐ Role-play with a friend or counselor serving as a stand-
in for the offensive person
☐ Mentally visualize better ways to handle similar events

I also suggest that my patients release their anger
through physical exercise and relaxation techniques.
Monica began taking walks along the beach and joined an
aerobics class.

When we are angry our bodies are tense and uptight. Releasing the tension through stretching makes us relax, and aerobic exercise releases "happy hormones" (called endorphins) that contribute to our sense of well-being. Racquetball, for example, is an excellent way to release anger. Some people prefer to work off their frustration through manual activities such as pulling weeds, cleaning the garage, or shoveling snow. Doing handwork, like needlepoint, may also be relaxing.

Devise your own plan of action:

To physically release my anger and relax, I will _____

_____

_____

After Monica had worked through these first four steps I confronted her directly with the underlying issue: "Will you let your baby go?"

I asked her to write a letter to the dead child, telling her how she felt. At first Monica objected, but after a little more thought she agreed to do it. That night she wrote a touching letter, which read something like this:

My dear baby Georgia,

I love you very much. Life has never been the same since you left. I live in hell now. I am miserable. I am angry. I have no reason to live. I am drinking myself to death . . . I just wish you hadn't left me.

Monica

That letter helped Monica release the anger that had been buried alive when little Georgia died. The hate was gone. Now she was ready to transcend her anger.

5. Transcend the Anger

Anger is such a powerful emotion that trying to deal with it in our own strength, without the supportive perspective of God's love, is very difficult. Even when our anger is effectively expressed, if we refuse to give up our feelings of hurt and rejection, the anger, like the Phoenix, will rise again. And the result could be even more devastating.

Forgiveness means giving up our pet grievances and frustrations to receive the grace to cope with the hurt in our lives. The apostle Paul encouraged us to "be kind to one another, tenderhearted, forgiving one another, just as God in Christ also forgave you."[2]

I believe prayer is an important part of forgiveness. I suggest choosing a very quiet, relaxing room with two chairs positioned opposite each other. The idea is to sit in one chair and imagine the person or persons who have hurt you sitting in the other chair. After recalling the painful feelings of how you were hurt, ask God to give you the grace to forgive the person as you mention his or her name. At the end of each prayer, commit yourself to treat that person with respect and love. As you move to forgive your spouse, your parents, your child, or your friend you will find a deeper appreciation of forgiveness and freedom in your life.

Part of Monica's therapy involved forgiving herself for responding to Georgia's death in ways that led to the breakup of her marriage. I always say, "Hurt people love to destroy that which they love." The destructiveness in their hearts vibrates out into their love sphere, injuring the people closest to them. Monica had closed her heart after the baby's death, pushing her husband away emotionally and physically. Her heart was so full of hurt and fear and sadness there was no room for love.

Monica carried guilt and shame over the divorce and believed God was mad at her. After she learned more about the character of God by studying specific Bible verses, she realized God had not abandoned her the way she imagined. She had been projecting her view of male authority figures onto God; her husband had walked away, so she believed God would too. Once Monica understood God's true character, she could trust His willingness to forgive her.

I recommend that patients read *Please Let Me Know You, God* by Larry Stephens of the Minirth-Meier Clinic for suggested ways of clearing away distortions in their image of God. Knowing God forgave her, Monica was able to forgive herself. For the first time she could enter her day with a clean slate and a clear conscience.

The day after Monica wrote her letter, I asked her if I could visit Georgia's grave with her. She looked surprised. Then she lowered her head and admitted, "I didn't even go to the grave at the funeral, and I haven't been there since then either." She told me that during the funeral she had walked out and left the priest with the corpse. Later he told her where the child was buried.

After much discussion Monica agreed to visit the grave with me. The next day I waited for her, wondering if she would come. She arrived at my office, dressed in black, and together we drove to a quaint churchyard cemetery. After a little searching we found the spot where Georgia was buried.

We stood in silence, then Monica fell to the ground, sobbing. "Oh, Georgia! Oh, Georgia! I really love you. I miss you. My life has never been the same without you. But I've got to let you go because, Georgia, I am so angry I am destroying myself. Good-bye, Georgia, good-bye."

6. Confessing Anger

Even after trying to express anger, we may still feel uptight. It may be helpful to find someone to talk to about the anger—not to draw additional support for your side of the argument, but to release the emotional burden still weighing on you. A trusted friend, priest, pastor, rabbi, counselor, or psychiatrist may be a good confidant. Make sure it is someone you feel comfortable with, someone who can keep things confidential. Here again prayer may further release the anger by directly confessing it to God.

7. Repeat Steps 1–6

Do not merely nod your head as you read these steps. Perform them. Talking about dealing with your anger and actually dealing with it are not the same. These suggestions can do nothing by themselves. They only work if you do the work.

And any time you feel angry about that particular situation recurring you need to repeat steps one through six again. Remember, dealing with anger is a process, not an event. If it recurs, we cannot ignore our anger and hope it will simply go away. What we do not work out, we will continue to act out.

Recently, I received an encouraging letter from Monica. She said, "I want to let you know I am not angry anymore. I have a good job; I've started my own company. I am no longer abusing alcohol. Thank you for forcing me to face the reality of letting Georgia go." Monica had been hurt. But Monica had also hurt other people. Hurt people hurt people. The final part of her recovery was to respond properly to those who were naturally angry with her.

You Are Bigger Than Your Anger

You have a choice. You are bigger and stronger than your inner anger—you *can* control it. Either you learn to deal with your anger or you allow it to burrow deeper into your heart and become organized as hate. Once that happens, your inner self becomes bitter and your basic attitude toward life becomes negative. As a result your heart becomes open to demonic or destructive behavior. The Bible warns, "'Be angry, and do not sin': do not let the sun go down on your wrath, nor give place to the devil."[3]

Scripture and psychology agree: If we don't learn to deal with our anger on a day-to-day basis, we are in danger of repressing it, creating bitterness, and inviting other destructive physical, emotional, and social problems.

We do have a choice. We can abandon destructive anger and instead choose to use anger constructively. Constructive anger allows us to establish healthy boundaries and use self-assertiveness. Constructive anger can also prompt courage and the development of community. Many people have defied difficult odds because they mobilized their anger to work positively for them. As Malcolm X said, "Usually when people are sad, they don't do anything. They just cry over their condition. But when they get angry, they bring about a change."[4]

Anger is the most destructive emotion. It can kill.

Often people let their emotions—or someone else's—control who they are and how they feel. We'll talk about that in the next chapter when we discuss your authority card.

✵4✵

Our Authority Card

If you had met Joan, you would have found her interesting and confident. Dependable. Charming. Yet she was hurting inside.

Joan confided, "I feel empty, useless, and my life is going nowhere." Joan was married to Stewart, a handsome macho guy who had come up the hard way. According to Stewart, "Life is tough and you have to work hard to make it." He was a well-to-do businessman, highly respected in the church, and known as a responsible citizen in the community. But at home he was tough and demanding.

Stewart was neat to an obsession. If the rug was dirty or if the beds were not made properly he would have a fit, telling Joan and anyone else present she was not a good wife. If Stewart did not like the meal, he threw a temper tantrum at the table. After an argument Stewart would threaten to leave. On a few occasions he actually did spend the night in a hotel in a nearby city. Joan would call every hotel until she found him and beg him to come home, promising she would be a better wife. Stewart would return and things would be fine—for a while.

Then he would revert to his old pattern of critical and domineering behavior—and again threaten to leave the marriage. The thought of her marriage breaking up terrified Joan. Divorce was unthinkable; she could not imagine herself as anyone other than Stewart's wife, a woman who colored the gray in her hair so she would look younger for her husband.

Then Joan started having panic attacks. With no warning she would suddenly begin to shake all over, become breathless, sweat profusely, and feel as if she were going crazy. At times her heart would beat so fast she thought she was going to have a heart attack. Sometimes the attacks would awaken her out of a sound sleep. Several times Stewart took her to the hospital in the middle of the night because she was experiencing such difficulty breathing. He was very concerned about her health, but the doctors could not find a physical cause for her condition. Joan was desperate and finally came to my office for psychological help.

I use a word picture to help clients like Joan understand why their lives are so miserable. "You have given your authority card to someone else," I say. "Human beings have inestimable value because they are made in the image of God.[1] This gives each human being what I call an authority card, an ID, a passport, that is the basis for his or her personhood."

The authority card gives each of us four inalienable rights: meaning, dignity, identity, and value (MDIV for short). This God-given authority card is your basic passport to satisfying relationships and a meaningful life. In the example above, Joan had given her authority card to Stewart, leaving no freedom in their relationship.

The one who holds the card calls the shots. The relationship is then bound by dependency and dominance, not love. People who give up their authority cards say they feel as if "a part of me is missing" or "my life is ruled by circumstances beyond my control." In contrast, healthy love is built upon the free exercise of choice and mutual respect; both individuals in the relationship maintain possession of their own meaning, dignity, identity, and value, their own authority cards. This chapter is designed to help you use your authority card in your own personal growth and discovery.

A Lost Authority Card

Some people go around collecting other people's authority cards and using them as credit cards to run up personal pleasures at someone else's expense, as Stewart did. He came to see me as he struggled to understand what was wrong with Joan. He understood the concept of the authority card right away. Tears came to his eyes as he admitted, "I've been holding on to Joan's authority card because I don't have one of my own. I sold myself to my career years ago, and the company still controls my card."

Stewart was right; his identity came from his "perfect" marriage and successful business. He had never walked through his own hurt trail, and he was smothering his pain with pride, as I had done before I walked my own hurt trail. His business card had replaced his authority card. We can't be too hard on Joan and Stewart though. All of us want to be led through the maze of life—if not by God, then by a parent-figure, a career, a social philosophy, or fate.

At times it's so much easier to let something or someone else make our decisions for us. But every time we give up our authority cards, we give up our power. Addiction takes our authority card.

Both Stewart and Joan had given their authority cards to addictions: Stewart to compulsive workaholism, and Joan to an unhealthy dependency on Stewart, a condition called codependency. Both of them were locked into this addictive relationship.

Addictions

The paralyzing pressure to keep up the right image (when one has no sense of intrinsic value and identity) is associated with addictive illness, whether the addiction is to drugs, alcohol, food, sex, or work. As one young girl explained, "When I gain two pounds, my world is shattered. I can't go out. I hate myself. Life is miserable."

A construction worker who has a busy schedule said that after working hard all day, he drinks a few glasses of wine to relax. Now his alcohol consumption and dependency are increasing and he admits, "My drinking is out of control. I feel burned out, but how do I stop? I must keep on working. I can't afford to slow down because of my financial responsibilities."

Similarly, cocaine use is enhanced by the perceived glamour of the drug. The prevailing image of our culture is to be cool, confident, and successful. In the early stages of use, cocaine gives the user the illusion of this image, almost as if it were specifically designed for our culture. As one young man said, "When I have my hit of cocaine, I get a powerful high. I feel in charge of the world . . . I am the boss! When I walk down the street, the road belongs to me. People move out of my way and make space for me. What a great feeling!"

Tragically, the crash always comes as the drug wears off. The promise of euphoria turns into dark despair and leads to a downward spiral of destruction.

Every addiction, even Stewart's workaholism, promises pleasure and self-fulfillment it cannot provide. Instead of the promised feelings of inner satisfaction, belonging, and significance, the end result is despair and dehumanization.

The cycle is predictable. It goes like this: Internal pain (a void, sense of inadequacy, love hunger, or loss) manifests itself as shame, anxiety, guilt, depression, anger, or boredom. The vulnerable person tries to alleviate this pain or comfort through some type of anesthetic—drugs, alcohol, relationships, work, rage, sex, food, or gambling. The anesthetic relieves the situation temporarily but later generates even more serious consequences—intense guilt, remorse, and dissatisfaction with the self.

Overwhelmed, the addict returns to the anesthetic in a deeper way, resulting in even more pain, conflict, and depression. Increasing doses of the anesthetic (drugs, work, sex, an unhealthy relationship) are needed to satisfy the person. In other words, enough is never enough; the "cure" (anesthetic) has turned into the cause of the pain. Eventually, the cycle spirals out of control, with the addict seeking even longer periods of anesthesia from the pain. It's hard to quit; you can't simply pull one plug and drain the swamp.

The attachment to the substance, thought, attitude, or behavior continues consciously and unconsciously even though the person recognizes it is destructive to his or her well-being. God-given meaning, dignity, identity, and value for oneself and others are lost.

The nature of the anesthetic generally dictates the speed of the cycle. For example, beer feeds the cycle slowly, while crack-cocaine works very quickly, throwing a person into the addictive cycle within hours. Eventually the addictive agent has a self-perpetuating life of its own.

Another driving force of the addiction is the withdrawal effect, which occurs when the addictive behavior is reduced or stopped. Withdrawal reactions, including irritability, anxiety, or depression, result when the brain reacts to the loss of the addictive substance. This reaction may be accentuated by the "cue phenomenon," something that reminds the brain of the addiction. In Stewart's case the cue was a messy house or a late dinner. At work, an unfinished project or a deal that was doomed to failure lowered his self-esteem even further. This led to a powerful craving effect that drove him to seek more of the addictive substance or behavior.

Another type of withdrawal reaction is the "rebound phenomenon," in which the addict experiences a reaction that is the opposite of the addiction effect. For example, after the use of a stimulant such as cocaine or amphetamines, the addict may go into a prolonged deep sleep followed by a depression.

In working with many different types of addiction, I have found that, alongside the techniques of group therapy and behavior programs, true healing occurs only when the addict recognizes a higher power that can act as an antidote to the imprisonment of self-gratification. Through worship of God, the Holy Other, a meaningful perspective is regained. Gratification can then be delayed and channeled to constructive means. The person regains his or her authority card by recognizing that he or she is made in the image of God.

George was a severe crack-cocaine addict. He was feared on the streets because he terrorized people and took whatever he wanted from them. He resisted every program for treatment. One night while he sat in his room feeling dejected, forlorn, and hopeless, he was visited by a young man who prayed with him and told him God loved him and came into the world to share his pain and struggle. At the end of the conversation George bowed his head and asked God for help. After joining a church, he enrolled in His Mansion, a Christian community dealing with troubled youth. There he received treatment, studied the Scriptures, prayed, farmed, and did woodworking projects with other people seeking spiritual community. Today George is married, has a child, and has been drug-free for six years. He works as a counselor helping addicts and troubled youth.

Similar stories have been repeated during my experience in the past ten years as I have battled the evil and destruction of crack-cocaine addictions. I have found that healing occurs only when addicts break their powerful narcissism to recognize a higher power outside themselves. Finding meaning beyond oneself emancipates the person from slavery to the cycles of self-destruction.

Distorted Perceptions of Reality

People who turn their authority cards over to addictions often adopt distortions—defense mechanisms that minimize the power of their addictions and their repressed hurt feelings and protect them from feeling pain. These distortions cause three main problems: confusing needs and wants, believing identity is based on possessions or feelings, and confusing vocation and career. In the following pages, we will look more closely at each of these common distortions.

Confusing Needs and Wants

The addicted person drowns the pain by focusing on his or her wants; then he or she converts these wants to needs as a way of rationalizing his or her behavior. This may even be true of addictive relationships. For example, Joan was devastated when Stewart insisted that they separate until she could get herself together. Because Joan was totally dependent upon others for security and identity, she began calling one friend after another for consolation and a security "fix."

When I suggested that her compulsion to call others was unhealthy she insisted, "I'm so emotionally upset I just have to call somebody! I need to talk or I can't handle it."

Not true. Joan did not *need* to talk; she *wanted* to talk because it fed her craving for attention and security.

Stewart also confused needs with wants. He had grown up in poverty and had worked very hard to become a successful businessman. Always mindful of his poor beginnings, he surrounded himself with expensive material possessions. Although Joan did not know it, he was sometimes sexually promiscuous, believing *It makes me feel powerful to be attractive to women.*

The truth was that Stewart did not *need* luxury items and the attention of pretty women to overcome the inadequacy he felt because of his childhood—he *wanted* those things.

In therapy Stewart worked on his personal hurt trail and was able to feel and express some of his buried hurt feelings and anger about his deprived childhood. He came to see that he did not need all of his boats, cars, or homes, and that he was destroying himself by trying to be a playboy.

When wants are translated into needs, we are catapulted into a roller-coaster experience where self-control is ignored in favor of self-indulgence. Before we go on, try to discern any confusion you might have about what you *need* and what you *want,* and think about how these beliefs are fueling your behavior.

First list the things you want. Then make a list of the things you really need.

In my own case, I listed these wants:

- A nice home
- A vacation each year in an extravagant environment
- A big sprawling library so I can pick up any book I want
- A media room with all the videos I want and a compact disc player that gives me great sound
- The best education for my children
- To spend every day on the Bahamian beach (There is a child in me that would like to let go and be free.)

Yet even as I listed these wants I realized these things went beyond the reality of my life; this forced me to look at what I really *needed*. I began clarifying my goals and my needs and wants through prayer, realizing I really didn't need a lot of the things I had wanted in the past. My list of needs was:

- A job that allowed me to exercise my professional talent
- A family to care for in a loving but not an extravagant way
- A reasonable vacation
- A simple compact disc player without all the gadgets and the media room
- A good basic education for my children

It is helpful to clearly identify wants and needs in this manner. Now it's your turn. Give yourself permission to be honest about what you want in life.

Things I Want:

1. _____
2. _____
3. _____
4. _____
5. _____

Things I Need:

1. _____
2. _____
3. _____

4. _____

5. _____

The items on your last list are the ones that will form your goals for the future. (In my case, the goal-forming needs were a job that allows me to exercise my professional talent and a family to care for in a loving, but not extravagant, way.)

Finally, select one of your goals and develop short-term steps toward reaching it. In my case, I chose as my goal the development of a meaningful professional life—a counseling practice and outreach work beyond my practice that allowed me to touch the lives of other people. The short-term steps I could take to realize that goal were:

- Writing a book like this to show the integration of my own personality and the process of discovery in my life
- Changing my style of writing from an academic to a conversational tone so I could express what I had experienced to a larger audience

Now it's your turn.

My goal is: _____

Some short-term steps I can take to reach that goal are:

1. _____

2. _____

3. _____

4. _____

My patients have found that doing this exercise helps them feel more in control of their lives. Human beings should think about their feelings and feel about their thinking. Let's apply that standard to a typical day-by-day decision.

Let's say you believe you have to wear a particular suit to project the right image. Now stop and think about that feeling: *Do the clothes make the man?* No. In the same way, you might think you have to have more money, so you add more and more work to your daily schedule. Stop and ask yourself: *How do I feel about this routine? Why am I making this choice?* This type of reflection helps you avoid confusing what you *have* to do with what you *choose* to do.

Believing Identity Is Based on Possessions or Feelings

Cultural aphorisms such as "You are what you possess," "You are what you feel," or "You are what you do" describe another distortion of the wounded heart. Tragically, if these attitudes are the source of our identities, our self-images are destroyed when we lose our jobs or something important to us.

The story is told of a man who built an expensive house on the side of a mountain. Warned that a mud slide was imminent after heavy rains, he refused to evacuate. Instead he sat on his front porch, drinking coffee. "All I have is invested in this house," he said. "I cannot live without it." He was what he possessed!

If I think I am what I possess, when I lose my possessions I am nothing. Or if I constantly think *If I get that extra degree or promotion I will be somebody,* or *I must get married to be a whole person,* if those things don't happen, I'm a nobody. Another thought distortion says, *I am what I feel, so I must feel good all the time. If I feel high, I must be great; if I feel depressed, I am bad.*

Rubbish. You are *not* what you feel. You are a person who has feelings.

The world's propaganda tells us, "Follow your feelings,"

and "If it feels good, do it." If you think about your feelings, however, you will realize it is often best not to act them out. What do you feel like doing to the driver who cuts you off on a freeway? What do you feel like doing on Monday morning after a busy weekend instead of reporting to work? It's hard to imagine any way our lives could be improved by following such impulses!

On the other extreme, feelings can be ignored or denied in favor of intellectualism. In some churches and families, there seems to be a belief that if you have a feeling you are in danger of acting out the behavior, so the prevailing sentiments are "We aren't going to have those feelings," "Don't get emotional," or "You don't really feel that way."

This faulty reasoning suggests that if you admit feeling angry, you will be in danger of lashing out. If you feel lust, you are liable to commit adultery. The attitude suggests feelings aren't safe because they get out of control. So an attempt is made to nip *all* feelings in the bud—if you deny a feeling or pretend you don't have it, then the feeling can't control your behavior. Right?

Wrong! Repressed feelings are more destructive than properly expressed feelings.

You don't have to live in fear of deep emotions. Instead, think about your feelings and feel about your thinking. To handle your emotions:

1. Feel the feeling
2. Then think about your response. You can always exercise self-control for these feelings as you can your anger.

Essentially, you are *more* than what you feel. Unlike animals, who experience a simple stimulus-response reaction, human beings have the ultimate freedom of the equation:

Stimulus + Choice = Our Response

We can choose how we will react to a stimulus. Thus, we are responsible for our decisions. Life does not have to be dictated by our feelings. Our personal choices can relate to a power higher than ourselves.

Some people let society do their (faulty) thinking for them. After all, it's easier. It's comfortable. If they give society the duty of solving their problems, they can blame society for everything that goes wrong in their lives without having to accept responsibility for the consequences of their choices. How handy! As a result they regress to primitive modes of ethical thinking and behavior. They accept such simplistic notions as:

☐ "Take care of number one."
☐ "I am sorry it is you, but I'm glad it isn't me. It's your problem."
☐ "The world needs to be nice to me because I'm (handicapped, black, female, or any other unalterable condition that is discriminated against)."
☐ "If you scratch my back, I'll scratch yours."
☐ "I am a product of my environment; if you give me better circumstances, maybe I'll make something of myself."
☐ "Serve God and you will be healthy, wealthy, and wise."
☐ "Believing in God should make me feel good." (Even God is now in the business of handing out better lives!)

Such cultural hogwash is in stark contrast to the life of Christ, who had to experience the cross, the crucible of suffering, as He served God faithfully. Jesus did not serve Himself; He served others and did the will of His Father. In this way He left us an example of emotional maturity.

The challenge is to recover the uniqueness of our real inner selves by working through the hurt and pain. In that way we become people who may chose to possess things or

experience a variety of feelings—without allowing our possessions, feelings, or work to define us.

Confusing Vocation and Career

Our identities are intimately tied to our professions, or
work. Upon meeting a person for the first time we often
ask, "What do you do?" The more wounded our inner
selves, the more vulnerable we are to take our identities
from our professional status. Retirement is extremely painful for these persons. I know a Christian gentleman who
has retired four or five times since he was in his middle
fifties. Now in his eighties, he is starting a new business
again to prove he can be a success. Obviously, his personhood is tied to what he does.

Accepting the difference between employment and vocation is an essential step in our search for the heart. By definition, vocation is the basic calling or responsibility of the
human being: to worship God, to use one's talents, and to
reach out in responsible love and service to family and
others. A career is only a means to that end. But in trying to
escape our inner woundedness, many of us try to make a
god out of our careers. When this happens, our careers
choke our vocations. Due to the pressures of time, materialism, and conformity, we allow our love to be choked out
by lies: *I have to go to work; I have no choice. This project
must get done.*

Wait a minute! Yes, you do have a choice! You can choose
not to allow a career (even motherhood or ministry) to become an end in itself. If it does, your vocation is destroyed
and, in the process, you lose your families, neighbors, and
friends.

When I was a medical student in Scotland, a wise older
man who belonged to my church told me, "Young man,
God has more to do *in* you than *through* you." His words

have never left me; in essence, he was telling me I needed to become a missionary to my own life before I could help anyone else.

What does this mean, God has more to do _in_ you than _through_ you?

A distinguished gentleman in Edinburgh was offered a new, higher position in which he would be paid a handsome salary for doing business around the world when he was fifty-five years old.

After much thought he turned down the job. He told me, "This job would be excellent for my career, but terrible for my vocation." His vocation (or purpose for living) included responsibilities toward his wife, children, grandchildren, church, and community, which would be hampered by this career decision.

When we are in touch with our authentic selves our choices are determined by the proper balance of vocation and career, not by what is bigger, more lucrative, or more powerful.

God does not insist that we be professionally successful. Micah 6:8 eloquently expresses the simple heartbeat of vocation: "And what does the LORD require of you but to do justly, to love mercy, and to walk humbly with your God?"[2]

We follow this "requirement" by appropriately appreciating ourselves, our families, and others; our work becomes only a part of our walk with God in the world. A preoccupation with career alienates us from the deeper experiences and fulfillment of life. Careers are temporal, while vocations extend beyond this life into the eternal meaning of love, faith, and hope.

Even a career of spiritual service can go sour. A very talented youth minister worked extremely hard to develop meaningful youth programs in his city. Gone day and night, he had no time for his family. As a result, his children grew up without him and did their own thing. Eventually, his two sons were expelled from college for stealing a cannon from the downtown area and, in a drunken stupor, dropping it from the top floor of their dormitory. Exhausted, the minister died suddenly of a heart attack. When asked why she did not attend her father's funeral, his daughter, who lived in a neighboring town, replied, "I could not afford to take time out of my busy schedule to attend."

An excellent career was allowed to destroy the vocation of this misguided man. Despite his work in the ministry, God and God's values were somehow left out of his own life. His authority card (containing his meaning, dignity, identity, and value) was misplaced.

By contrast, people who are comfortable with their own God-given values and identities are not threatened or controlled by the world's perception of their career successes.

During my first year of psychiatric residency at Harvard, I had the opportunity to listen to several nuns who had decided to leave their religious work to enter secular service. Perplexed, I asked to speak to the Mother Superior. I wondered how she felt about the nuns leaving the convent. The Mother Superior gently explained that she had joined the convent to accomplish her mission of serving God. She continued, "If God chooses to show me that working at the convent no longer serves my mission, His will be done. I will continue to carry out my mission in some other way. If God calls my sisters somewhere else, they should go there to serve Him."

This dear lady of God was saying her vocation came first—and that could occur in the convent or outside of it. And she extended that freedom to others. The secret of this woman's security was her deep faith in God and her commitment to worship and serve Him at any cost.

Joan's Authority Card Became Her Discovery Card

In seeking identity in her husband's approval, Joan had made him into an idol, a pseudo god. And the more she worshiped at his throne, trying to please him, the more demanding he became. Her greatest fear was that Stewart would abandon her; she was unconsciously panicking at the thought it might happen. In therapy she shared her pain and honestly faced her fear of Stewart's leaving and her own inadequacy for the first time. She came to realize her sense of meaning depended upon her acceptance of herself as a person in her own right.

Joan began to understand that even though she was living in a dysfunctional family, she had her own authority card. All the words she had heard growing up in church now took on a personal significance as she realized *she* was made in the image of God and *she* was special. Joan had God-given meaning, dignity, identity, and value. Her authority card became her discovery card for the abundant life.

Joan had to relearn the meaning of love: a mutual sharing relationship that allows the identities of both partners to remain intact and be enhanced. Describing this process, she said, "I started coming alive again. I began to feel that I am somebody."

Now I was ready to talk to them together in joint counseling about their addictive relationship—and suggest a better way.

Using Your Authority Card in a Relationship

Falling in love tends to occur in two phases. In the first phase the strong emotional attachment (chemistry) creates a sense of ecstasy and oneness. There is great togetherness with some likes and dislikes and each trying to please the other. It is as if the couple has regressed to the early stage of mother-child fusion. If the relationship is to mature and develop, as the mother-child relationship does, differentiation and boundary formation occurs. This leads to the creation of distance and reestablishment of the partners' identities as individuals as well as a couple.

Let me share a beautiful story of two friends who were the ideal love-story couple. They lived in Cambridge when I was at Harvard. Whenever you saw her, you saw him; when you saw him, you saw her. After a fire in their apartment building, the newlyweds needed a place to live, so I invited them to stay with my wife and me. Whenever I came home from work, this couple was in each other's arms or on each other's laps or eating from the same plate.

The husband eventually got his first job. After his first day at work he brought home champagne and roses. When I asked, "What are you guys doing?" they answered, "We're celebrating our reunion after being separated for eight hours."

One night I came home and found the husband sitting outside on the porch. He was angry and sad.

I asked, "What's happening, eh?"

"Well, you know, she's different now. She's getting bossy like my mother. Before, when I suggested we do something, she would agree. Now we're just fighting all the time. I don't know if I love her anymore."

I thought to myself, *The dawn of reality!*

I went inside and found the wife crying. When I asked what was wrong she told me, "He's really getting difficult. He's not like he used to be. He's so stubborn, just like other men. And I don't know if I love him anymore."

Relieved, I called them in and we talked about what was going on. I said, "Relax. The honeymoon is over; fusion is broken. Now you can decide whether you will choose to love each other."

Every marriage relationship or friendship eventually

reaches this second phase, where we have to *decide* to love each other. Love is a choice. As Scott Peck writes, "Love is the will to extend the self for the nurture of one's and the other's spiritual growth."[3] Mature love is the decision to move toward the loved one—even when it is easier to pull away.

Love is a nurturing relationship that requires time, patience, and fortitude. Love does not exist apart from ambivalence and periodic mistrust; it exists in spite of these sporadic feelings.

The test of any truly loving relationship is the development of the spiritual virtues such as trust, truth, beauty, faithfulness, forgiveness, acceptance, tolerance, and commitment. Contrary to the cultural belief, love does not relate to possessions, sensationalism, or sexual prowess.

So often falling in love involves fusion; it's like being connected to that other person by an umbilical cord. And it's great. It's oneness. But as differentiation occurs and we separate, we have to look at each other—and we have to *choose* to love. Instead, there is the temptation to think, *I loved you, but now we're not like we used to be.* At this point Hollywood says, *Look for another lover.* In truth, love requires both separate identity and unity.

Similarly, in a very deep sense God has *chosen* to love us. At times we will experience closeness in our relationship with Him and with each other, but many times we experience distance. It's our choosing to love that allows us to act in loving ways and with loving attitudes toward God, ourselves, and each other.

True intimacy between two persons is possible only if each person has undergone the separation-individuation process. The more one has a sense of self, the closer he or she forms an intimate relationship with another. True discovery leads to intimacy.

In my concept of intimacy, a meaningful relationship

with another person is enhanced by having the love of God as the apex of the relationship so that when problems rise the transcendent relationship with God acts as a bulwark, a source of strength.

Yet true love between two persons can sometimes be distorted. Next we'll look at two common relationship problems: fear of engulfment and strong dependency needs.

Fear of Engulfment

Closeness becomes difficult when a person fears engulfment—being dominated, trapped, overwhelmed, or absorbed into the life of the other. As a result distance is deliberately created, and that leads to a fear of abandonment.

Janet and Jerome loved each other. Janet, very talented, self-directed, and self-assured, came from a family where she learned to express herself without reservation. Jerome, on the other hand, was reticent, a little insecure, and found it hard to express his feelings. He loved Janet deeply. However, when Janet expressed her love to him, he found it hard to reciprocate. In closeness he froze and became insecure. As a result, lovemaking was brash, unplanned, and completed as quickly as possible.

Recognizing this problem, Jerome became depressed and felt distant from Janet. Feeling guilty for not being able to express himself, he feared Janet did not love him and would leave him. This further accentuated his fear and isolation. As a result he did everything possible to make it up to Janet.

Jerome recalled that when he was six years old his father left his mother for another woman. This was very painful for Jerome, especially because his dad did not contact him after the divorce. He remembered seeing the other kids' dads picking them up from school and hearing them brag how their dads took them on hikes, played football with them, and helped them build projects at home. Nights were the most difficult time for Jerome; he dreaded going to bed. As he lay there the pain would start in his abdomen and move up to his chest as if a heavy load of brick were pressing down on him. Terrified, Jerome would pull the blanket over his head, hoping the pain would go away. Going under the blanket was like going away from the pain.

As Jerome expressed his pain over the loss of his father, he cried and started to shake. He agonized over unspoken questions such as, *How could my father do that to me? How can I let myself love anyone else and face abandonment again?*

In essence, he was afraid of closeness because of his fear of loss. Because of being rejected by his father, in his heart he had mixed feelings about becoming close enough to be hurt by anyone else. Tragically, in avoiding closeness with the one he truly loved, he was opening himself up to more pain.

Seeing this connection between rejection by his dad in childhood and his current problems in being close to his wife allowed Jerome to get in touch with his hurt inner person. As he was able to do the grief work, he became increasingly free to be close to his wife. There was no quick fix, but it did open the way to the healing of the marriage.

Strong Dependency Needs

Another intimacy problem occurs when a person has such dependency, or love hunger (an extreme need for love that was never satisfied as a child), that he or she clings in relationships, draining or exhausting the other person. Often such a person comes from a socially and emotionally deprived home where he or she did not receive appropriate love and support from the parents. This may be because the parents were dead or because the family experienced some severe tragedy.

George was a very weak, dependent person. He was married to an attractive woman who found him boring, empty, and draining. When George learned that his wife had had an affair, he was deeply hurt and turned to alcohol. When his wife left him, George went to pieces. In therapy, he developed close relationships with the men and women in his group. Confronted about his strong dependency needs, George was challenged by the group to be more assertive and take responsibility for himself. He shared how he had been very close to his mother who had been overprotective of him during his childhood. She was always there for him. He came to see that his strong attachment to his mother had been transferred to his wife, who found it exhausting, draining, and too demanding.

Working through his pain, George became increasingly responsible for his own behavior and more assertive in the group. The support group's love and caring gave him a sense of acceptance and a place to work through his strong dependency needs. He now enjoys healthier friendships, has stopped drinking, and is doing well in his job.

As Joan considered her dependency on Stewart she determined to change their codependent relationship. About six months after she and Stewart had reconciled, Stewart came home to find the house messy and the evening meal not ready. He began to get very angry and said he was leaving the marriage.

Although she was nervous, Joan sat up straight, braced herself, and said, "Stewart, I love you very much. I really want our marriage to continue. But if you have to go, please go. I want you to know I will not fall apart. God loves me, He is with me, and I am special. I know I can make it. I will survive."

Stewart was shocked by Joan's answer. This was a new Joan! The punch line is that Stewart never left home again. And Joan is now a responsible homemaker—because *she* wants to be.

Conferring Personhood on Others

True self-actualization should always lead us to others. That is, the more I understand myself, the more I discover my need to relate interdependently with others. Each person holds his or her own authority card. Each person has meaning, dignity, identity, and value and therefore must be treated with respect. We help other people grasp their authority cards, we confer personhood on others, by the way we treat them. This became obvious to me years ago when I was a Kennedy fellow in medical ethics at Harvard.

As a Kennedy fellow, I was asked to give my ethical opinion about the quality of life of Debbie, a baby girl who had been born severely retarded, with a poorly developed brain; in classical medical language she was hydroan encephalic.

Unfortunately, her mother felt as if the baby's physical deformity was her fault, and the father was a brilliant academic who also blamed the mother for Debbie's condition.

Her medical treatment was questioned when Debbie developed pneumonia. Some doctors suggested supportive treatment to make the baby comfortable but giving her no antibiotics; this course of action would allow the baby to die. "Let nature finish its course," they proposed. Others considered the baby a person, and as a person, they said, she should be given antibiotics, the basic care any human being would receive as treatment for pneumonia. We all knew a situation like this could have consequences for the medical care of future patients.

It is amazing how young people like myself jump in where angels fear to tread. I agreed to give my opinion. Yet as I began visiting this child each day and talking to her parents, a very eerie feeling came over me. Was I doing something totally inappropriate? Who was I to make a decision about who was or was not a person? What was a person anyway? I began to feel as if *I* were on trial.

As will often happen, a reporter heard about our dilemma and asked permission to visit the child. I escorted the reporter to the baby's room one afternoon, and as we were climbing the stairs to the second floor of the hospital we heard singing.

As we neared the door to the ward, the words became clear. "Happy birthday to you. Happy birthday to you. Happy birthday, dear Debbie, happy birthday to you." Five nurses stood around the baby's crib, singing to her.

I turned to the reporter and said, "Well, they gave her personhood, didn't they?"

Later, when I asked the nurses why they had celebrated the baby's birthday, one of them replied, "Dr. Allen, we don't know all the ethical, philosophical arguments, but this child is one year old today. We sang "Happy Birthday" because we love her. We appreciate her. And that's what we do for our own children."

"Your simple gesture spoke very deeply to my heart," I said. "You helped me realize that human beings, made in the image of God, can confer personhood on other human beings by the way we treat them, by the way we respect them, by the way we love them."

Even though she was treated with antibiotics Debbie died because the prognosis for her abnormality was very poor. But now, years later, I still remember that I, too, can confer a meaningful personhood on other people by the way I greet them, the way I smile, the way I relate to them with honesty and respect.

Each of us has an authority card. Each of us has meaning, dignity, identity, and value. As we realize our value, we need to look back at our past and see the love stories that were there all along, hidden by the pain in our hearts. That's what we'll look at next.

❧ 5 ❧

Our Love Story

I was brought up in a traditional home where the concept of caring from the heart was demonstrated by my parents' love for their children and others. They were not perfect, but in their own way they taught us to love from the heart.

I will never forget my mother's sending me to take tomatoes from our farm to widows who were not as fortunate as we were. And when I was thirteen years old she encouraged me to start visiting Mrs. Rolle, a ninety-nine-year-old woman who lived across the street.

At first I was apprehensive, or perhaps the better word is *terrified*. I'll never forget the first Sunday I visited the old woman in her two-story house that had once been white but was by then almost gray from age. I walked up the concrete steps to the porch, which was sloped and rickety due to the rotting wood. A dark curtain covered the door. The house was spooky, which added to the rumors that the old lady had dealt in witchcraft.

I knocked softly. Maybe no one would answer. But the door opened slightly and a woman greeted me who was probably Mrs. Rolle's granddaughter. The hallway behind her looked dark and foreboding.

"I came to visit Mrs. Rolle," I said. After looking at me

with a Why-are-you-visiting-her? look, the woman led me into a tidy but dark living room, with an old rug in the center. Mrs. Rolle sat in the corner. Her face was wrinkled but she looked regal in her long white skirt and sweater and her neatly combed hair. I introduced myself, but there was no reply.

I tried again.

Still no answer.

Finally I realized she might not be able to hear me, so I leaned close to her ear and spoke very loudly. Her eyes told me she had heard my introduction, but when I tried to talk further with her, I received nothing but a blank stare.

Mother had told me to chat with her and then read Scripture to her. Since I couldn't get her to talk to me, I decided to follow Mother's second suggestion. I opened the Bible I had brought with me and began reading the Twenty-third Psalm. "The Lord is my shepherd, I shall not want. . . ."

As I continued I noticed Mrs. Rolle's mouth moving in sync with what I was reading. Then I heard a slightly audible sound, a mumbling of the beloved words: "He leads me . . . He restores my soul. . . ."

Encouraged by her response, I continued even louder. "Yea, though I walk through the valley of the shadow of death. . . ."

Mrs. Rolle nodded her head as I read those words as if she were agreeing with me. Then her voice joined mine, finishing the rest of the verses loudly and clearly: "I will fear no evil. For Thou art with me."

We had found a common ground. Only a few minutes after the psalm was completed, Mrs. Rolle began talking to me. "I'm very, very old," she began, acknowledging the respect her seniority granted her, "but I have a lot of sins."

I didn't know what to do. She was an elder and I was a child, with milk still on my mouth. What were the sins she was talking about? Then I noticed that this frail, ninety-nine-year-old lady had tears in her eyes. I knew she must be thinking about something very painful. I wanted to comfort her so I told her about Jesus' love for her. "He forgives us when we sin," I said.

My mother had taught me the one thing you could always do for someone was pray—so I prayed a simple prayer, asking God to forgive the old woman. "Lord, bless this dear lady and help her to feel better about herself. Forgive her for whatever happened." Soon after that I shook her hand and said good-bye.

Every Sunday afternoon after that I visited Mrs. Rolle. I usually read a portion of Scripture, most frequently the Twenty-third Psalm. In the next months she smiled more and obviously began to look forward to my visits. Her family helped her onto the porch each Sunday afternoon so we could talk there together.

As time went on I felt more and more comfortable and safe with her. I knew she must have learned a lot to have survived all those years. I soon began to feel as if I was getting much more than I was giving.

I will never forget one particular Sunday three years later, when Mrs. Rolle was 101. That day she asked me to come close to her. Then she put her hand on my head and prayed softly, "God, bless this young man." It was a sacred moment.

The next Tuesday as I was riding my bicycle home from school I saw a hearse parked outside her home. "The old lady died this morning," our neighbor said. I had lost a real friend.

I leaned my bike against the rickety porch and went into the house. There I met Mrs. Rolle's minister, the Reverend Talmage Sands, a very sophisticated, handsome man who was well known in the islands.

"Boy, I know your old man," he said. "We went to school together." He looked at me and chuckled. "In fact, I beat him up one time. I've heard you have been visiting Mrs. Rolle. I'm so happy you are carrying on your dad's tradition of caring for other people."

Then he said something that really shocked me. "You know, I am her minister, but you have *really* been her minister. You have visited her every Sunday for the last three years. You should do the funeral, not me." I couldn't imagine that he was serious. After all, I was only fifteen! Yet the next Sunday I stood beside Mr. Sands, looking out at the people who had gathered for Mrs. Rolle's funeral in a very big church in Nassau, the Zion Baptist Church on Shirley Street.

Mr. Sands told the huge congregation about my visiting this elderly lady. Then he turned to me. "If anyone should speak at this service, it is David," he said.

I don't remember my exact words, but I told about my love for Mrs. Rolle and how her heart opened when we first read the Twenty-third Psalm together. "My mother encouraged me to visit her," I admitted, "and in some sense maybe I helped her. But I also received a special blessing from Mrs. Rolle. She taught me a lot about life—a tremendous respect for old people, for one thing, and the meaning of faith and the power of Holy Scripture for another. At 101 years she was more secure in her faith than she'd ever been before. She knew her sins had been forgiven and God loved her. Although we were separated by almost ninety years, an entire lifetime, we were one at heart."

Mrs. Rolle taught me that Scripture is a common ground and prayer is a gateway to the presence of God. I, in turn, led her to inner healing and spiritual serenity. Was that psychotherapy? Or was it just caring, or simply the way of island life? I don't know if there is a right way to describe the process of working through past guilt and hurt to embrace an invitation to love in the present moment. I do know we touched each other's hearts.

What began as a sharing of our family's Christian love from the heart became a significant love story in my own life. I was willing to listen to my mother, who had an intuition—or a leading of the Holy Spirit, as some would say—that I should spend time with this old woman. In doing so I received a great gift, a blessing that has lasted a lifetime.

The Love Story

When we say the word _love_ we automatically think of romantic love. Many of us remember the movie _Love Story._ Yet, as you can see, the love story I am talking about here is not necessarily romantic love.

Once we have worked through our hurt trail and our anger, and we have freed our hearts of the poisonous feelings that held them captive, we can look back at our lives and see God's presence and guidance in the midst of our pain. We can see the love that was previously blocked by the painful emotions, times when people were very kind, times when we were able to serve someone else, times when a beautiful sunset was a powerful statement.

Our love stories are the holy moments of our lives when we felt God's love and the love of those around us. As we look back we see how God's love was expressed; then we look at the present and see how His love continues to be expressed. Those stories give us hope for the future: God's love has been there in the past, is present now, and will guide us in days to come.

Your Own Love Story

Your childhood memories will also contain significant positive events that helped make you who you are today. I encourage you to think about these times so you can get in touch with the power of affirmation and love in your life.

Life is a mixed blessing. Any approach that refuses to acknowledge the positive or dwells on the negative will not lead to healthy discovery. The seeds of love and truth are often planted at the moment the heart is cultivated to receive them.

I always tell my patients to write down moments of encouragement or blessings from their past. In my own lovestory journal I listed my friend Mrs. Rolle, the lady who lived to be 101. I also listed Liz, a nurse tutor in London; she was a caring woman who was dying of cancer. I met her while I was working at Guys Hospital in London as part of a summer internship rotation. I was asked to "clerk" Liz, to write up her history.

As I was talking to this sophisticated blonde woman who spoke with an elegant English accent, I felt an unusual presence of joy and hope. After my usual rounds, I went back to talk to her again, and Liz told me that once you have cancer, time seems to expand and lengthen.

"You appreciate people more," she said. "Once I was afraid to hug my older children. Not now. I realize I am counting my weekends, counting each day, as you say," she explained. "And yet we all need to count our weekends since life is fragile for all of us. We are all passing through life in a transitory way. Cancer just speeds up that reality."

Yes, the pain was there, she told me. Yes, the pathos was there too. But paradoxically the quality of her life had deepened and improved. "My life has slowed down," she said again. "A day might seem as long as a year to me now. My life has become pregnant with meaning. People mean something. Flowers mean something."

I always left her room feeling thirsty for that quality of life. She was pushing me to look deeper into the concept of discovery. The model was there in her experience. Liz had worked through her hurt trail, her cancer. She had cried about it. Then she had asked herself, _What's life all about? What do relationships really mean? How can I grow in the few days I have left?_

I admired her fortitude, her spirit, her determination—it was contagious. Liz gave me a love of psychiatry, a medical specialty that allowed me the opportunity to spend time listening to other people's hearts as I had to hers. It's a sacred specialty because it allows me to walk within the inner chambers of a person's heart and sit there in awe. And in a very deep sense any time I walk into someone else's heart I'm also walking into my own and learning more about myself.

That which is most personal is also most universal. In our hearts we are one, you and I and Liz and John, the Boston man who launched me on my journey of discovery with the velvet harpoon. That was my second love story. In the same way, you will be able to look back over your life and recognize people and events that impacted your life for good.

Now it's your turn. List your own love stories below:

1. _____

2. _____

3. _____

4. _____

5. _____

6. _____

Now take your four most positive love stories and fill in your age when the experience occurred and the persons involved:

Experience	Age Occurred	Persons Involved
_____	_____	_____
		_____
_____	_____	_____
		_____
_____	_____	_____
		_____
_____	_____	_____
		_____

Now list what you learned in each of these four experiences.

I filled out this portion of my love story like this:

Experience	*I Learned*
Visiting Mrs. Rolle, my elderly friend.	The power of Scripture. Ever since then the Twenty-Third Psalm has been very comforting to me. I have also studied King David, the writer of the psalm, and his experiences. After all, if he could write a psalm thousands of years ago that would speak so eloquently to a young boy and an elderly lady, he must have known a great deal about God's love.

Now it's your turn:

Experience	I Learned
_____	_____
	_____
	_____
_____	_____
	_____
	_____
_____	_____
	_____
	_____
_____	_____
	_____
	_____

Now look at those same four experiences and ask yourself: "How did it enrich and fulfill me—now and then?"
First I'll show you how I answered this question.

Experience	Fulfilled Me Then
Liz's life	The greatest blessing to me was to be able to help her by listening to her. That deeply touched me.

Fulfills Me Now

At the time I did not understand the power of empathic connection at all; she taught me how to listen heart-to-heart. As a result of that experience I decided to go into psychiatry.

The blessing Mrs. Rolle gave me so many years ago in the Bahamas has also stayed with me. I will never forget one Sunday afternoon when I was in medical school in Copenhagen. It was four o'clock, the same time I used to visit Mrs. Rolle. I was very lonely, so far from home in a country where I could not speak the language. A mental picture of Mrs. Rolle came back to me; I remembered her giving me that blessing, and it nourished me. At difficult times in my life, when I've been very lonely, her blessing has given me fresh impetus and encouragement.

How did your experience fulfill you then and how does it fulfill you now?

Experience   Fulfilled Me Then

_____

_____

_____

Fulfills Me Now

_____

_____

_____

Experience

_____

Fulfilled Me Then

_____

_____

_____

Fulfills Me Now

_____

_____

_____

Experience

_____

Fulfilled Me Then

_____

_____

_____

Fulfills Me Now

_____

_____

_____

Experience

_____

Fulfilled Me Then

_____

_____

_____

Fulfills Me Now

_____

_____

_____

Now ask yourself, "How can that affirmation better prepare me for resistance in the future?" First you'll see how I answered the question.

Experience	Prepares Me to
Blessing from Mrs. Rolle	*Keep going when times are tough. I feel God's blessing around me.*

Now it's your turn. How does each of your love stories better prepare you to face resistance in the future?

Experience	Prepares Me to

Negative Experiences Can Also Be Love Stories

Believe it or not, I also listed as one of my love stories John, the Boston heroin addict. As you consider your own love stories, look for times when a painful remark or an embarrassing incident actually worked for good in your life or rechanneled your efforts. Some of life's best medicine initially tastes bitter, like cod liver oil.

I remember another patient, like John, who challenged my approach to psychiatry. She was a doctor's wife who was sent to me by her internist because he believed she was complaining about pain that wasn't really there. "Her cancer is in remission," he told me, "so she has no reason to be feeling this pain. Maybe she is depressed."

After I talked to this woman for a while, I decided her internist was right. She was depressed. I suggested that she take an antidepressant.

"No, no," she protested. "I don't want medication. I'm not depressed. I tell you I'm going to die, and I'm naturally upset to leave my husband."

She sighed with impatience. "I want you to talk to me about spiritual things. I know you have a faith. I understand you speak in churches and have a Sunday school class."

I found myself getting very defensive. "Well, you know," I said, "I'm a psychiatrist. I'm supposed to evaluate your physical and emotional health, not your spiritual health. And your internist tells me you are in remission. It looks like your cancer may be much better. You're not going to die."

"No, no," she protested again. "You're going by pure medical facts. I'm telling you that I'm not going to live very long. What I really need is some hope or meaning in life. If you can't give me the spiritual help, then I'm going to your brother-in-law; he is a pastor and will give me the help I need."

Two months later this woman was dead. Her funeral was perplexing to me. As I looked at her lying in the open coffin, her words came back to me: *I came to you because I needed spiritual help.*

I felt bowed by her plea. *What am I all about?* I asked myself. *Does the patient really know what he wants? Maybe if the patient says she wants spiritual help, I need to give it.*

Too often I find myself in a psychiatric box, trying to pull away from the spiritual nature, even though I believe in spiritual discovery. Yet my patients are searching for meaning. And cancer patients are particularly anxious to talk about the spiritual nature of things. Unless addressed, maybe patients could fall off a cliff spiritually, just as we worry about their doing so emotionally.

Pure psychiatry approaches life from a bio-psycho-social perspective. At Harvard I came to know B. F. Skinner and his behavior model. I also studied the stages of cognitive moral development with Professor Lawrence Kohlberg, and at the same time studied Professor James Fowler's stages of spiritual development. More and more I began to realize these philosophies needed to be integrated. In psychiatry we need a bio-psycho-social-*spiritual* perspective.

That lovely woman, dying of cancer, had been talking to me about the core of life. Now I know I should have stopped and listened to her heart. I should have taken off my psychiatric blinders. Instead I lost that opportunity—for her and for myself.

Her funeral became a love story for me because I realized again there is more to life and healing than textbook psychiatry. There's a lot about life we don't know or understand. And it became very clear to me again that discovery is a process. Even though I had walked through my hurt trail and opened my heart, I sometimes forgot to think and listen through my heart. I had failed to listen sympathetically.

Each day I realize the love story means standing and looking at the mystery of life, perhaps admitting, "I don't understand it. I don't have to. But I can appreciate it. And I can accept the times I fail."

List two negative experiences that were love stories:

1. _____

2. _____

Why did these experiences turn into love stories?

1. _____

2. _____

I have found that Romans 8:28 is true: "All things work together for good to those who love God, to those who are the called according to His purpose."

Now think back to the experiences in your hurt trail. Was God there in the midst of the pain?

_____ Yes _____ No

List the experiences from your hurt trail that turned out to be a love story:

1. _____

2. _____

3. _____

You might want to take a few days to complete this exercise so you can ask relatives and others about specific details. You might also want to look back through family albums and other pictures.

Finally, go back through each of these events and specifically thank God for every aspect of the blessing you received. Share your positive emotional response with Him just as you shared the pain of your hurt trail. The life-changing power of the love stories in your life is often neglected when the focus is on recovering from past hurts. It is as important to acknowledge and learn from these tremendously positive incidents as it is to work through your hurt trail.

Setting the Love Story Straight

When we look at the suffering in our world and the problems in our lives we may be tempted to think it's too hard for one person to make a difference. We give up on our own love story, and we repeat the negative patterns of the past.

Sometimes we fail to think with our hearts, as I did. Then the final love story is to accept our weaknesses. One love story in my life has become a symbol of the ups and downs, the successes and failures, of my discovery process.

It is a special memory that stands out about my father, a kind man who loved the soil and worked extremely hard. A rainwater tank with a cement cover stood outside our home in Nassau. The extreme heat of the Bahamian sun cracked the concrete, and my dad, being a handyman, repaired the crack again and again.

But after each repair the sun would eventually open the crack up again. This was very frustrating to him. Finally he accepted that he was unable to repair it. Instead he filled the crack with soil and planted tomatoes. The seeds germinated and he weeded them often with his machete, watching with satisfaction as they produced huge, red, juicy tomatoes.

This became a powerful parable to me. So often the most difficult thing in life is to face the truth about ourselves and our situations: We are flawed, and there are some unrepairable cracks in our competency. Although there are many things we can fix and should make every effort to, other things must be accepted. How beautiful it is to accept our painful imperfections and our cracked world and use them to bring about something beneficial or beautiful. Instead of yielding to frustration and despair, we can plant our tomato seeds as my father did.

Late in the evening on August 22, 1979, I called my father. He talked with me about my work and my life, and he encouraged me to return to the Bahamas to help build my country. The following morning, while I was making rounds on the teaching ward at Yale where I was the director, I received word that my father had died. Apparently that morning he had risen early and gone out to weed his tomato plants. He had a heart attack and was found dead with his machete nearby. To the very end of his life, he was a model of faithfulness and love. As a man lives, so he dies.

How shall we then live?

The next part of this book answers that question. It explores the model of living Christ gave us at the Last Supper and describes seven attitudes of the heart that encourage and direct us in our search for authentic identity, intimacy, and meaning in life.

❧ PART TWO ❧

Attitudes
of the
Heart

❦6❦

A Spirit of Grace: Love

Ted and Nelly were a middle-aged couple who deeply loved each other. In the last few years, now that their children were raised, they had been able to enjoy each other's company as never before. They played golf together, walked together, and traveled together when Ted's business trips took him to interesting places. Each knew no one cared about him or her as the other did.

Then tragedy struck. Nelly had a stroke that left her paralyzed, with only one functional arm. Unable to talk, she mumbled angrily under her breath. She never smiled. She would not even extend her good arm to Ted in love. Her hurt, disappointment, and despair destroyed the joy once present in their home.

Needing an outlet, Ted visited a hostel for orphans, where he met Jason, a disfigured little boy whose mother had burned his arms and shoulders with a hot iron in a fit of anger. Ted brought the boy home for a visit and left him in the room with Nelly. When he returned Jason was sitting on his wife's lap with her good arm around him. His wife was crying as she gently caressed the little boy.

When Ted took the little boy back to the hostel later that afternoon, the child asked him why Nelly could not speak. Learning of Nelly's stroke, the child began to cry, saying, "I am sorry your wife can't talk." The tough husband could feel tears coming to his eyes for the first time in months. When he returned home he went into his wife's room, and they held each other for the first time since her stroke. The love of a little boy unlocked the love in the hearts of the paralyzed woman and her husband.

Nelly's despair over the helplessness and hopelessness of her stroke had filled her heart, leaving little space for love, beauty, and truth. However, the little orphan boy whose pain was so obvious by the withered red scars on his arms and shoulders broke through Nelly's wall of pain. She opened her heart so she could again feel the love around her.

The Process of Discovery

Nelly's illness led her to see her life as finished. Because of her disability she had to look for meaning within the limits of her disability—and also beyond. In a very important sense, a lot of life means saying good-bye. Nelly had to learn to say good-bye to a healthy body.

The minute we are born we begin the process of saying good-bye. When we leave the womb, we say good-bye to the safety and security of being perfectly fed and nurtured. This is probably the hardest thing we do in our whole life, so it's a good thing we don't remember it! Every good-bye represents a microcosm of our own death.

The Last Supper is particularly significant to me because in today's psychotherapy terms it was the Lord's "termination" session with His disciples. He wanted to tell them good-bye before he went to his final test, the cross.

All good psychotherapy eventually leads to a termination session, but it is one of the hardest phases of my work, a time when the therapist and the client both feel anxious. Sometimes the client doesn't come for the termination interview. Sometimes the therapist doesn't show up. This happens because both are having trouble saying good-bye, partly because it's a form of dying, and partly because so much needs to be said to conclude a relationship or experience.

Our Lord really wanted to tell His disciples what was on His heart at the Last Supper. He was telling them this was the heart of His ministry, the heart of the meaning of His life here on earth. In other words, "Listen to Me carefully because I really want to share with you what My whole purpose in coming to earth was all about."

He outlined a process that gives life meaning and hope, and leads to a life that goes beyond the issues of this world. The eight steps described in the rest of this book outline a process of utmost seriousness because they deal with our saying good-bye to the losses of life—and saying hello to the meaning of life.

In this chapter we will consider the first step, love.

The Healing Power of God's Love

Whether it is carefully orchestrated or springs forth as a response to the unexpected, the first and basic step to discovery is love. We must be open to the sustaining power of God's love, the creative, redemptive, healing force of life.

At the Last Supper Christ made it clear He loved His disciples. He reminded His disciples that regardless of what happened, God's love would continue to reach out to them. "He loved them to the end."[1]

As I began working in psychiatry I became very disillusioned. The more I studied, the more I realized how important love is to a child, particularly a mother's love. All babies begin as totally dependent human beings. It is a sobering thought to realize we are alive only because someone was there for us when we were infants. Someone loved us.

Supported by the stability, consistency, and predictability of the mother's care, buttressed by the love of the family, a child grows into a loving and caring human being.

But what about a child who doesn't receive his or her mother's love? So many kids don't have that experience. Can they ever love—or be loved?

Life seemed very deterministic to me. Using this set of facts you could almost gauge what would happen to a person. If a child didn't have a good enough mother and a good enough family, his or her life would be blasted forever. If a child didn't *have* love, that child couldn't *give* love. And if love was necessary for healing, many of my patients' prognoses were totally hopeless.

Searching for an answer, I found it in a totally unexpected place: the Christian concept of love, a concept I had been taught as a child but never integrated into my work.

My life had been fragmented into three distinct areas: my work in psychiatry, my faith, and my social concern. One person went to church on Sunday, another person worked in psychiatry during the week, and yet another person devoted extra hours to helping people who had little money to help themselves—three seemingly unrelated persons existed within me.

Then, when I was looking for a way to help my patients learn to love and be loved, I realized that human love, from a Christian perspective, is based on God's love. And God's love fuels human love. If my patients hadn't received love as children, they could still get it—and give it—by opening their hearts to God's love.

Life then made sense to me. There *was* hope. Even if a child didn't have a secure family or the love of a mother, God's love for that child was unchallenged. His love could still heal those who would open their hearts to receive that love. And through His love hurting persons could meet other people who could also share His love—and help them. Christ "loved them to the end," and He promised His disciples His continued love and provision. In reality, then, Christ was telling His disciples that regardless of what happened to them in the future and no matter how their lives had been messed up in the past, He would be there for them. Intentionally, not accidentally.

So, too, if we are going to move to discovery, we need to love by design—deliberately opening our innermost selves to accept love, even when pain seems to overcome us. Love is not just a sense of feeling ecstatic or walking in nirvana. Love is a result of the commitment to work through the pain and hurt in our lives, as we did in Chapter 2, so we can open more space in our hearts to love, beauty, and truth.

Unfortunately, we sometimes substitute distorted love for the real love of God.

Distorted Love

When We Love Our Problems

Janice was a pleasant, hard-working mother who consulted me because she was very worried about her son, who was deeply involved in drugs, had failed in school, and showed no interest in developing a career. Overwhelmed by feelings of guilt and failure, Janice resigned from the church choir, an activity she had enjoyed for many years, and withdrew from the church entirely. In a deprecating and hopeless tone she stated, "My world has collapsed, life has lost its zest, and I have nothing to look forward to. I even find it hard to believe in God."

After listening to her for a number of sessions, I recognized an increasingly vicious cycle of despair, depression,

and hopelessness. Janice had developed a pathological fixation on her problems with her son. During one session I
broke into her litany of guilt and despair by asking, "Has it
occurred to you that you have made the problem with your
son your god?

With surprise she asked, "What do you mean?"

I explained that any problem that is allowed to occupy all
our waking and sleeping moments, resulting in our withdrawal from faith, personal development, and supportive
community, has become our god. And by definition, God is
so powerful and encompassing that any problem of that
magnitude is unsolvable. Even if the particular problem
were solved, it would leave such a vacuum that another
problem would quickly take its place.

The woman was having a destructive love affair with her
problems. "In essence, you are sacrificing yourself at the
throne of your problem, your god, and in the process you
are being destroyed," I explained.

"What should I do then?" Janice asked in amazement.

"What do you want to do?"

"What do you mean?"

"Well, you have two choices. You can either take away
the god status of your problem and reestablish your faith, or
you can continue to worship your problem as your god and
destroy your faith, the very force for life and meaning."

The issue was one of perspective. As human beings
made in the image of God, we can convey god-like status to
any person, place, or thing by loving and worshiping it. The
apostle Paul described this situation when he wrote, "Because, although they knew God, they did not glorify Him
as God, nor were thankful, but became futile in their
thoughts, and their foolish hearts were darkened."[2]

If we love the attention we receive by talking about our
problems or the adrenaline rush a crisis brings or the identity we gain by being associated with some big tragedy,

then the love story of our lives becomes destructively distorted.

Sometimes it's scary to see how deeply our hearts can be deceived. The issue of godship is a predominant theme in the psychotherapy of behavior. Overwhelmed by circumstances beyond our control, we tend to invest problems with such psychological energy that they usurp the place of worship in our lives and gain gripping power over us. The result is dehumanization, depression, burnout, and in some cases, self-destruction.

Remember:

1. You are not your problem. Don't let your problems define you.
2. God is bigger than your problem. Don't let your problems become your God.

The importance of perspective—keeping God, ourselves, and our problems in rightful proportions—is stressed throughout the discovery process. But we live in a world of lost perspective. In our confusion we often focus on ourselves. We become our own god.

Destructive Self-love

Love is distorted when we worship projected images of ourselves: our needs, our wants, our abilities, our potential, our accomplishments, our status. This is perhaps the single greatest obstacle to discovery.

Enhanced by aggressive marketing techniques and undergirded by a powerful philosophical psychology, this fixation on the self is a harsh taskmaster. We struggle to achieve the right look, the best health, the proper job, the appropriate house, the perfect image. I do not mean we should neglect our self-esteem or fail to work toward a positive self-image. But when self-image relating to bodily appearance, mental superiority, and power over others becomes an end in itself, we become enslaved by narcissism; perfecting ourselves becomes our purpose for living.

All around us we find individuals who have become what one counselor called "balcony people," people who act out their lives as if they are on stage—with one eye always glancing up to the balcony to see if others are gently applauding. Rather than living by convictions and values, the balcony people's actions are chosen to ensure that others approve, admire, and sympathize. They strive to manipulate their love stories rather than loving from the heart.

Balcony people choose the role—martyr, caregiver, daring adventurer—that most pleases their target audience. Life is ruled by what they think others will think of them. Not surprisingly, balcony people suffer from the constant pressures of "performance anxiety" and self-promotion. They are narcissists.

The modern word *narcissism* comes from the Greek legend of Narcissus. According to the classical Greek myth, Narcissus was a handsome young man, and all the nymphs constantly threw themselves at him, hoping to get his attention. But the arrogant, beautiful Narcissus ignored their overtures and was totally absorbed in himself. Looking in a pool one day, he fell madly in love with his reflected image and tried in vain to initiate a relationship. When he reached out to make contact, the water rippled and the image disappeared. And at evening, though he begged the image of the handsome youth to stay, it refused and went away. Rejected and forlorn, Narcissus wasted away from unsatisfied desire and was transformed into the flower that bears his name.

In Greek, *narkissos*, the name of the beautiful plant with showy yellow or white flowers, is traditionally connected, by virtue of the narcissus plant's narcotic effects, with the word *narke*, meaning "numbness, torpor." Hence the word *narcotic*, a substance that blunts the senses, causes euphoria, and when used habitually can be addictive. Thus, the association of narcissism and addiction is clear from the root of the word.

In psychiatry, a narcissistic personality is "a personality disorder characterized by extreme self-centeredness and self-absorption, fantasies involving unrealistic goals, an excessive need for attention and admiration, and disturbed interpersonal relationships."[3] This inordinate love and preoccupation with one's self is also characterized by a lack of interest and empathy for others—in spite of the pursuit of others to obtain admiration and approval.

S. M. Johnson, in his book *Humanizing the Narcissistic Style*, describes narcissists as people who "are too busy proving their worth—or more properly disproving their worthlessness—to feel the love, appreciation and joy of being human."[4]

The self-centeredness that is distorting the perspective of individuals around the world comes from our hurt trail, which we have already discussed.

While talking about the wounded inner child is currently in vogue, I prefer to talk about the wounded inner person. I have met many persons who have had a very secure childhood experience and were strongly protected and supported through many painful experiences. But somehow things went bad for them in later life—a broken marriage, a child with great potential who messed up, the death of a loved one, or the abrupt end of a promising career. We are wounded in childhood *and* in adult life.

To compound the problem of the pain in their past, children being raised in our Western culture have come to expect so much materially in life that self-gratification becomes the expected and accepted norm. Without a true focus on the worship of the Holy Other, we are totally thrown upon ourselves to become the captain of our ship and the master of our fate. This enormous responsibility forces us to become our own god. But God is all powerful and all knowing. Therefore, to be our own god, we have to know everything, win every battle, and be in total control. This of course is ridiculous. And eventually we find ourselves angry, burned out, fatigued, and depressed.

The only cure is God's love, a fact I realized years ago in East Boston with John. Love is an act of the will. We *choose* to discover love by actively accepting the love of the Holy Other.

The Holy Other

Psychiatrist Gerald May wrote:

After twenty years of listening to the yearnings of people's hearts, I am convinced that all human beings have an inborn desire for God. Whether we are consciously religious or not, this desire is our deepest longing and our most precious treasure. It gives us meaning.[5]

While on a lecture tour in Argentina, I met a wealthy woman who told me she had been a severe cocaine addict. When she came to the end of herself, having lost all faith and trust in her ability to find healing for her addictions, she grabbed a lamppost outside her home and prayed to it daily. She claimed that putting faith in this lamppost helped her.

Then, while lecturing in Miami, I met a quiet, withdrawn young man who told me he had been a cocaine addict and had messed up his college education and destroyed the trust between him and his family. Feeling isolated, discouraged, and deprived, he said he needed something beyond himself. In desperation, he started to pray to a chair. He said, "I had to find a faith, a higher power." Both of these examples show people coming to an end of themselves and seeking strength in a higher power. But what a sad commentary on the nature of their false gods!

If I asked you to close your eyes and picture a small boy with dark hair and mischievous eyes, you could do so. And you could take it a step further and imagine a conversation with that boy, noting both your comments and what you perceive his response would be if he acted in character. Those would be real and possibly powerful thoughts, but the boy would not be real—even if you sincerely believed a real boy would act that way. It would only be an invented image, a composite drawn from your knowledge of what boys look and act like.

For some persons, the higher power they envision and worship—like the child above—originates within themselves. And these persons, no matter how sincere their belief, find themselves crushed when their god image is powerless and unable to exert influence in the world.

By contrast, the Most High God who created the universe is transcendent. That is, God exists above and beyond our thoughts of Him, our constraints of time and space. God can therefore act in our behalf.

Through faith in Christ, God's spirit resides within us, yes; but it does not stop there. God inhabits the entire universe and is sovereign over heaven, earth, and human hearts.

When we unveil our hearts we find we are much in need of help, comfort, unconditional love. We need the Living God, who fully comprehends our hurt trail, yet can lift our lives above the limitations of our past or the sorrow of the present. God's love is not bounded by the physical limits of disease or death.

Discovery is finding the transcendence of God, love, joy, and inner peace that exists apart from our circumstances. Where there is love there will be pain. The love of Jesus led

Him to suffering as well as to joy. He was a Man of sorrows, familiar with suffering because He cared about us so much. As I reach for God's love, I often ponder the hurt trail of Jesus, the One who was fully God and fully man.

Christ's Hurt Trail

Watch with me as the Lord looks at some of the stops on His hurt trail—a trail He endured for you and me, even though as God He could have rejected it.

1. Whipped until His back was raw from the open cuts
2. Made to carry a heavy wooden cross miles through the streets of Jerusalem and into the hills beyond
3. Nailed by the hands and feet to the cross He had carried and left to die a slow, painful death after hours of suffering

Now think about the persons who hurt the Lord and what He should have expected from them:

Hurt	Person	He could have expected
Death on the cross	Judas	Love and loyalty. Judas was His disciple.
	Sadducees	Respect and fairness.
	Peter	Love and commitment. He promised to stick with Him at all costs.
	Pharisees	To be treated justly, according to God's commandments.

Christ endured this pain because He loved us. We can think of His love as we walk through our own painful experiences. In my view, it is impossible to deal with the woundedness in our own lives unless we are entwined in a cocoon of God's love. Hence the words, "He loved them to the end" have special meaning because they remind me that regardless of how bad things become, God's love envelops me.

It is God's love that breaks through the universe and sustains us. It is God's love that gives us the "I" in our lives, giving us a sense of ourselves and allowing us to hold our authority cards. It's simple, it's basic. It allows us to stand with confidence and say, "I am because I am loved."

Because Christ loves us to the full extent, we can afford to explore the meaning of our lives. I tell my patients, "You are called to the mission field of your own life, which includes your hurt, your pain, your broken marriage, your messed-up kids, your lost job. Once you commit yourself to face the pathos of your mission field, you will find the grace and healing of God's love waiting there for you."

Everything in life is created twice—first in the mind of the creator and then in reality.[6] If you are going to build a building, you conceptualize it in your mind, then you make it a reality. We imitate what we have learned by experience—even if that experience is suspect. Whose blueprints are you following in your life? Your mother's? Your father's? Or do you live in a codependent way with society around you?

The love of God in our lives means we are made in His image and therefore we have the authority to draw our own blueprints, write our own scripts. In that script we can choose to imitate the model of love Jesus provided for us; we can develop our personal mission statement and then see it created.

In his book, *The Seven Habits of Highly Effective People*, Stephen Covey makes the point that many of us follow a middle-management design for our lives and thus avoid leadership. Management is clearing the jungle; leadership decides which jungle to clear. Management is painting the building; leadership decides which building to paint. Discovery means writing your own script, not just copying the patterns around you. It means choosing your own plan, not improving upon someone else's. What tragedy to be clearing the wrong jungle or painting the wrong building. Instead, lead your life to love.

Discovering Love Through Liberty

Noted Scottish scholar William Barclay wrote this about the Passover Feast of the Last Supper:

> The Passover Feast was a commemoration of deliverance; its whole intention was to remind the people of Israel of how God had liberated them from slavery in Egypt. First and foremost then, Jesus claimed to be the great liberator. He came to liberate men from fear and from sin. He liberates men from the fears which haunt them and from the sins which will not let them go.[7]

Victor Frankl came to appreciate his personhood in the concentration camp. In so doing he moved away from being reactive and became proactive. He realized that even though his captors could destroy him, they could have no power over his freedom to respond, his basic attitude. In essence, this meant his captors had power over him, but in their spirits they were less free than he was. Victor Frankl discovered the liberty to love that no one can deny.

You, too, can discover more about love if you spend time

in reflection this week. Devote a section of your journal to the love in your life. Keep in mind that the love story is an ongoing process; it is not limited to childhood events.

What does it mean to you to know that God loves you and that you can never be away from His presence?

In my journal I recorded a time when I returned from work, drained and feeling as if I had failed to help a client. I threw myself down on the sofa in my study and looked out at the sea. I remember thinking, _God loves me_, but that seemed so trite; it was something I'd known all along.

I began to realize that maybe I had difficulty giving and receiving love because I had a restlessness in my heart. I realized I knew more of God's holiness and His law, but it was very difficult for me to bask in His love. I remember sitting there, the sunshine coming in through the picture window, repeating that thought over and over again, _God loves me. God loves me. God loves me,_ and I found a sense of peace. All I had to do was to be faithful.

Now it's your turn:

Write an account of a time you have felt particularly loved or close to someone.

_____

_____

_____

What factors led to such a meaningful experience?

_____

_____

_____

Obviously you should look for other experiences where these factors are present!

Think of a time you were especially encouraged through the act of nurturing someone else. Here's what I wrote:

I remember Dr. Mendez, a short, serious, but pleasant doctor who had come to the Bahamas to retire because he was fed up with the rat race of a practice in a big North American city. He began attending my Sunday school class and the Sunday evening group at my house, Seadance.

At first he would sit quietly whenever we prayed, but I always had the sense that he was listening and working through his pain. Each Sunday night we would go to my library and he would ask to borrow books dealing with spirituality and Christianity. He was a voracious reader.

One Sunday night he broke his silence with a simple prayer, "Oh, God, thank You for being with us."

In the following weeks he seemed to be happier. He asked to volunteer at Knowles House, our rehabilitation center for drug addicts. I noticed how he served these people as a volunteer. A man who had been a medical doctor for thirty years seemed to now be content with working as a support person, a quasi social worker. Because of his work there, he was asked to join the staff of Sandilands Rehabilitation Center, the major mental health center of the Bahamas. I felt as if I had helped Dr. Mendez find some meaning to his life.

Now it's your turn. Think of a time when you were especially encouraged through the act of nurturing someone else:

_____

_____

_____

_____

_____

_____

What things keep you from extending yourself toward others? Here's what I wrote:

This question always puzzles me because at times I can be extroverted, but at other times I am quite shy. There have been times when I would really have liked to extend myself, but didn't. My shyness kept me from it: my fear and my uncertainty.

What keeps _you_ from extending yourself?

_____

_____

_____

Opening your heart to love not only gives you a sense of being loved by God, but also an appreciation of your life and intimacy with someone else. The love of God also opens you to the discovery of the beauty and glory of God's creation, and the beauty of nature, in turn, inspires you toward more openness in worship and love.

Gertrude Stein said, "A rose is a rose is a rose." But in discovery language, a rose is _more_ than a rose. It is a symbol, an expression of God's love, the recognition that _I am loved! I have meaning!_ God the Creator continues His creative work, bringing beauty and love into the world. The beautiful, delicate rose and the beautiful, delicate heart are His handiwork. So are our acts of kindness and love.

One Christmas when we were sitting around the table

where we discussed cases at the Mental Health Center, Dr. Mendez told me a story filled with God's love.

"I was a captain in the German army during the Second World War, stationed just outside Moscow. It was Christmas Day and the troops were celebrating, so I volunteered to take sentry duty. As I walked through the snow on that cold day I reflected about what Christmas meant: peace on earth. I realized I didn't know what that really meant, especially here.

"I suddenly noticed an enemy soldier; he had his back to me so he couldn't see me. He was within firing range. In a moment I realized it was my duty to shoot him.

"I cocked my gun to fire—but I found myself feeling uneasy. And I found myself praying. *O God, I do not know who You are or if You even exist. But it is Christmas. And I don't want to shoot this man. Maybe his life will be meaningful in the future. Maybe he has a wife or child back home, waiting for him. . . . Maybe, God, You could show me someday who You really are so I could know You.*

"I did not shoot.

"After the war I went to medical school, emigrated to America, and went into practice, but I always had that longing to know God. My prayer was answered at your home forty years later. Through your teaching and fellowship a sense of faith developed in my heart. I've found it's easier to believe in God than not to believe in Him."

Little did I know when I first met this man that a powerful discovery was going to take place. And I don't know all of the story even now. What happened to that soldier? Is he still alive? Has God spoken to him in a special way? I do not know.

I do not know your story, either. But God does. My prayer for you was written long ago by the apostle Paul.

That Christ may dwell in your hearts through faith; that you, being rooted and grounded in love, may be able to comprehend with all the saints what is the width and length and depth and height—to know the love of Christ which passes knowledge; that you may be filled with all the fullness of God.[8]

7

A Spirit of Oneness: Communion

When my son, David, was fourteen we went for a boat ride in our fifteen-foot Boston whaler to Rose Island, a beautiful island of the Bahamas just a little way out from Nassau. I planned the excursion to be one of those delightful father-and-son outings you read about in books.

Life has a way of interrupting our intentions.

From our home it's about eight to ten miles out to this small, beautiful island where we were supposed to meet some friends. David and I were enjoying the rolling waves and the sun glistening off the aquamarine waters of the Caribbean as we headed out, relaxing in the pleasure of being together. All of a sudden we heard a loud thud as if something had hit the motor. Then the comforting whirl of the engine stopped. I looked at the water off the starboard side but couldn't see anything that might have gotten caught in the motor. The engine had just conked out, and we were left without power, miles from shore.

I couldn't get the motor to turn over manually, and we were drifting so I hurriedly threw the anchor overboard. Then I went back to work on the engine to see what could be done. But nothing I did seemed to work. As a nonmechanical person I began to feel a little panicky.

As I turned to look at David I noticed the anchor rope was not attached to the bow. In my hurry I had thrown the anchor overboard without securing it! Our motor was broken. We had no anchor. And we were drifting in forty feet of water farther and farther away from Rose Island. Those beautiful, gently rolling waters looked wild and treacherous now.

Yet as David and I realized our predicament we couldn't help laughing. Finally he said the obvious, "Daddy, that was a stupid thing to do." (I'd heard those words before, but this time the voice was filled with love and acceptance—despite what I had done.)

Somehow, even though the situation was dangerous and seemed hopeless, we felt better because we were together. We tried paddling with a little oar but the more we paddled, the more we drifted away from Rose Island. So we gave up and just sat waiting for someone to rescue us. Even though the situation was completely out of our control, it seemed okay because we were together.

From time to time inner accusations surfaced: *I was stupid. I was to blame. I wasn't thinking. I had endangered my son. I was a helpless psychiatrist who couldn't fix an engine or tie on an anchor.* (There was some truth in those thoughts! The great sack race was not all that long ago.) But my son communicated acceptance of me and the situation I had gotten us into, so I was able to discard those old thoughts of failure. I was also able to accept my frail humanity and proneness to do absent-minded things on occasion. My own process of discovery freed me to appreciate the positives of our relationship without panicking about our situation or feeling insecure about my failures as a man and father.

After a while we saw a bigger boat about a half-mile farther out in the sea and we tried to flag them. Either they ignored our plea for help or they didn't see us. Ten minutes later we saw a smaller boat, manned by two young men, heading in our direction.

As they came alongside, they asked what had happened. "We don't think we can pull you all the way back to Nassau. Our boat isn't that strong. But we can take you to one of the beaches at Rose Island."

We had been headed to a beach on Rose Island to meet our friends so I assumed they might still be there. It's a chance we had to take. It took us an hour and a half to travel the five more miles to get to that particular beach. As we came toward the dock I saw a few boats I recognized. We were safe.

You can imagine how difficult it was for an islander to live down doing something that silly at sea. As the story got out, the joke among my friends in Nassau for a long time was, "Dr. Allen, do you need an anchor?" (My reply was that I needed two!)

But even in a potential crisis, David and I remained close. Our communion with one another sustained us.

Too often, we do not know how to exercise self-control under stress so we can maintain closeness despite the problem, or we don't know how to open ourselves to the needs of others when we are also needy. We get stranded in life's deep water and don't know how to be the loving, caring individuals we want to be. And we miss out on the joy of communion.

The Necessity of Communion

We were created for communion; it is a basic requirement for meaningful human relationships. In Genesis, the

Book of Beginnings, it is written, "It is not good that man should be alone."[1] As a result God gave man a helpmate for companionship and fellowship—for communion.

Communion implies that we are not alone. I mentioned earlier that it is not the pain in childhood that injured our hearts, but the sense that no one supported us through that pain. Communion—community—gives us that support. Community helps us have the courage to reflect on our painful feelings and then open our hearts to love. David's and my life were somewhat threatened by our hazardous jaunt to Rose Island, but the pain—the fear of the dangers that arose—was lightened by our communion. Community is an essential step in the path to discovery.

Throughout this discussion I will use the word *communion* in a broad sense, meaning the sharing of ourselves with others. The concept of communion here is meant to imply and include:

- The act of sharing significant thoughts, feelings, and moments with another
- Sympathetic conversation
- Fellowship and companionship
- Connectedness and belonging
- A spiritual sense of oneness

Communion at the Last Supper

The communion of the Last Supper encompasses all of these elements. Christ was sharing much more than a meal with His disciples that night. It was their last meal together before the test of the cross. It was the Passover feast, a Jewish celebration in which they remembered their miraculous deliverance from Egypt after the sign of the lamb's blood on the doorposts of their homes had saved them from the angel of death. In a very deep sense the Passover represented the identity of the Jewish people, giving them cohesion, fellowship, community, and hope for the future.

And from Christ's perspective, it was a time to look forward to what God would do in the future. He knew He would soon have to walk the way of the cross. He said, "I have desired to eat this Passover with you before I suffer; . . . For I say to you, I will not drink of the fruit of the vine until the kingdom of God comes."[2]

He was saying, "We're in this together. Regardless of what happens, My love will be stronger than death."

During their time of fellowship at the Feast of Passover, Jesus instituted the first Communion, or Eucharist feast. Partaking of the bread, He said, "Take, eat; this is My body."

Then He took the cup, and gave thanks, and gave it to them, saying, "Drink from it, all of you. For this is My blood of the new covenant, which is shed for many for the remission of sins."[3]

His body was to be bruised and broken and finally destroyed for the healing of the world. His blood was to be shed for the atonement of humankind's flawed nature and sinful behavior.

And He asked His disciples to continue this tradition in memory of Him. Like the Passover feast, Holy Communion is a reminder that in spite of the ambivalence and tragedy of life, the kingdom of God has dawned.

Because of God incarnate there is a basic faithfulness at the core of life:

- Love has overcome hate.
- Good has overcome evil, and
- Hope has overcome our despair.

Communion also represents the close bond between Jesus and His followers. They are one. How important this truth can be to our mental health! My son and I did not withdraw from each other or irritate each other. I did not turn on myself, blaming myself for being at fault. We refused to let our circumstances ruin our relationship at the very moment we most needed each other. But without a release from past hurts and an openness to love (the first attitude of the heart), people are not free to approach life this way.

So many persons are seriously hurt and abused because no one reaches out to help them. As one lady who was asked to recall the pathos of an earlier trauma said, "It was so very lonely. I felt all alone. Nobody was there for me."

I feel that the communion service is essential to discovery. After my mother's death I attended a communion service at our church before the funeral at 3:00 that afternoon. As the minister repeated Christ's words, "Take, eat. This is my body given for you," I began to realize I was communing with the living Christ, now, at 8:30 that Sunday morning.

In the heart there is no sense of time. Christ's words in that communion service spoke directly to my heart, as if He were standing there before me. I shared the communion with Him that day. And as I did I remembered that He said, all those who believe in Me are in Me. I felt that I was also sharing communion with my mother. That comforting experience gave me added strength to face the funeral later on that day.

The communion experience is not optional but mandatory for anyone seeking spiritual discovery since Christ is the center of our spiritual development. As we become bonded to Him in communion we also become bonded to ourselves and others.

The Eucharist is also a sign of thanksgiving. As we gather to partake of the bread and wine, we are expressing our gratitude for the kindness and love of Christ in His sacrificial death. In a recent biography of Picasso, the artist is quoted as saying that his intention was to bring the Absolute into the frog pond of life.[4] And to that end he said he failed. Using Picasso's word picture, the Eucharist is a reminder that the Absolute, God in Christ, came to be with us in our frog pond.

Beyond remembrance, community, and thanksgiving, the Communion gives us hope that our pilgrimage makes sense. For Christ Himself said He would not celebrate the feast again until the fulfillment of the kingdom, when faith has given place to sight and we know as we are known. Communion is both a remembrance of what happened in the past and a prophecy of true communion with Christ when we will be with Him forever and ever. Now we are with Him in Spirit. Then we will be with Him physically. And then we will know all aspects of ourselves as never before. We will find out who we really are.

Discovery, the process of helping persons reach their potential, is intimately involved with fourfold communion—with God, with ourselves, with others, and with nature.

Communion with God

Regardless of how busy our Lord was here on earth, He always took time to spend with God, the Father. This was the hallmark of His ministry. In the midst of meeting people's needs for healing and deliverance, He would arise and depart into the mountains to pray. Christ said people "ought to pray and not lose heart."[5]

Prayer is two-sided. Prayer is the Holy Spirit in us relating to our hearts, and prayer is God calling us to communion with Himself. Prayer completes the circuit between us and God, giving us hope and direction. Prayer is opening our hearts to the prayer of God taking place in our lives.

Feasting at the dinner table of fellowship with God requires arrangement and preparation. We have to plan our lives to find the space and place for prayer. Regardless of how busy Jesus was here on earth, He always found time to pray.

I was brought up in the structured way to say my prayers when I went to bed and in the morning when I got up. After I began to understand a little about prayer I began to agree with the idea that prayer is "practicing the presence of God." Prayer occurrs any time I stop and focus on God's presence, whether it be asking Him, *Please help me to know this patient's needs,* or saying to Him, *Lord, thank You for the beauty of this sunrise and the peace of this early morning.*

I still pray in the morning, but my prayer is more a promise to open my heart to God during the day. I ask God to be with me as I see patients during the day. *Show me Your presence through them.*

Prayer is not just talking to God but opening ourselves to Him, seeing the whole world pregnant with His presence.

Prayer is almost like psychotherapy, with God as our Counselor. In therapy, people open their hearts to their psychiatrists. But even when they have done this, they can't express certain things because they are either too deeply hidden inside the heart or they do not wish to share those things with anyone else. Yet many of my patients have shared these deepest thoughts with God in prayer and found healing.

Prayer starts changing our hearts so we are open to God's love. Thomas Keating, a Cistercian monk at Saint Benedict's Abbey, said:

> Through the regular practice of contemplative prayer the dynamism of interior purification is set in motion. This dynamism is a kind of divine psychotherapy organically designed for each of us, to empty out our uncon-

scious and free us from the obstacles to the free flow of grace in our minds, emotions and bodies.[6]

Yet sometimes the fearful thoughts whirling around in our heads and the noise of life around us are so loud we cannot hear the Spirit praying within us. Then I like to remember the verse: "In quietness and confidence shall be your strength."[7]

One person described it in this way: "In the early days of my faith, prayer was mostly petition. But in seeking a deep experience of God and the spiritual healing of my inner life, prayer became waiting in the presence of God. The assurance was that He knows what I need. Thus prayer essentially is communion with Him."

Once we open our hearts to the presence of God, He prays through us. The apostle Paul told the Roman Christians, "The Spirit Himself bears witness with our spirit that we are children of God. . . . The Spirit Himself makes intercession for us with groanings which cannot be uttered."[8] There are certain things, such as suffering, we don't understand, and prayer allows God to pray through us, to take the deep hurt feelings of our heart away so we can open our hearts to love and joy. I believe Christ prays for us, even when we may not be aware of it.

I often use the following model for my own prayer time:

1. Choose a quiet space
2. Read a short portion of Scripture. Repeat it regularly for five minutes. Think of its application to you. (I often read Psalm 23, a favorite of mine, or Isaiah 41:10. This focuses my heart and settles it. I also memorize familiar verses of Scripture.)
3. Remain still, listening to your breathing for a couple of minutes.

4. Praise God for His greatness and marvelous creation.
5. Thank Him for the gift of your life.
6. Confess your failures and ask for forgiveness.
7. Express the feelings of a particular hurt that is bothering you.
8. Remain silent for two minutes.
9. Give your hurt up to God and forgive the person who hurt you.
10. End by singing the Lord's Prayer or the doxology.

The challenge of prayer is to move beyond the mere intellectual exercise so that prayer comes from the heart. When I was teaching at Yale, Father Henri Nouwen told us of the Hesychast tradition in which monks repeat the Jesus prayer: "Lord Jesus Christ, Holy Son of God, have mercy upon me." As they repeat it hour after hour, day after day, this prayer sinks into their hearts and becomes automatic. Then their prayers become like breathing. They occur without ceasing—in their waking moments and in their sleep.

If prayer is communion with God, the Alpha and the Omega, the Supreme Force of the universe who controls all events in our world, then prayer gives guidance, instills hope, and counteracts anxiety and fear. The apostle Paul wrote:

> Be anxious for nothing, but in everything by prayer and supplication, with thanksgiving, let your requests be made known to God; and the peace of God, which surpasses all understanding, will guard your hearts and your minds through Christ Jesus.[9]

Communion with God, our Higher Power, is a watershed experience that enhances communion with ourselves. Being made in the image of God, the more we connect with Him, the more we accept ourselves and reflect His image.

Communion with Ourselves

Before Christ left the world, He told His disciples He would send the Holy Spirit to comfort them and lead them in all truth. The Holy Spirit is in our lives, relating with our hearts. This eternal relationship gives us the courage to face all parts of ourselves.

Through worship we become a symphonic community so that all of our parts, adequate and inadequate, accepted and rejected, pure and shameful, form a unity within us. One becomes complete in Christ. David describes this in the Psalms when he says, "Unite my heart to fear Your name."[10] So often we forget that community _without_ is a reflection of the communion _within_ the person.

Henri Nouwen talked about three movements of the spiritual life in his inspired book, _Reaching Out._[11] Understanding those three movements, from loneliness to solitude, from hostility to hospitality, and from illusion to prayer, will help us understand the importance of communion with ourselves.

From Loneliness to Solitude

The first movement of Nouwen's three movements is from loneliness, the experience of feeling totally abandoned, to solitude, being at peace with oneself. A person who is lonely, restless, and insecure seeks relief in anything to break the sense of being isolated—telephone calls, alcohol, gossip, and even destructive behavior.

Solitude requires the development of the self so one can be nourished by the memories of past meaningful experiences, rather than frantically seeking new experiences. Solitude requires reducing the noise around us to hear the true music of our hearts. It means moving beyond the pangs and craving for human contact to listen to the voice of God, or, as someone has said, to hearing the music of angels. Solitude is the deep spiritual awareness that "You will keep him in perfect peace, whose mind is stayed on You."[12]

Enjoying moments of solitude is a sign of true communion with God and ourselves. We become comfortable, as psychiatrists say, "thinking about our feelings and feeling about our thoughts." This communion centers on being rather than doing. It is processing our lives: counting blessings, mourning past mistakes, and simply praying for others. It is meditation on the splendor of God and His creation.

From Hostility to Hospitality

Nouwen's second movement of the spiritual life is from hostility to hospitality. From childhood, most of us have suffered multiple losses, rejections, or different types of abuse—our hurt trail. Because of the inability of our caretakers to be there for us, many of these hurts have been repressed, as I mentioned in Chapter 3. Unresolved, they have turned our hearts into infernos of hostility that separate us from each other. Yet our hearts thirst for communion, as Helen's did.

Helen was distant and disinterested toward others. She described growing up in a cold home with an abusive father and a very cold mother. She spent most of her time hidden away in her room, burying her hurt and anger in secret, and feeling sorry for herself. She described her life as a dark tunnel and herself as being ugly, fat, and obnoxious. Because she hated herself she would even tie herself up as a means of punishment.

Though Helen was brilliant at school, her anger was diverted into academic supremacy, especially over the boys in her class. She had no friends. Eventually Helen met a woman who shared the Judeo-Christian belief that God loved her. The woman showed Helen how this love was validated in Christ's incarnation and redemptive sacrifice of love. Feeling strangely moved, Helen went through a religious experience in which she was intellectually and emotionally constrained to seek a deeper meaning to life. Her resulting faith gave her a desire to welcome others into her life. She became a very good teacher who had a deep love for her students, especially underprivileged children. She underwent the deep spiritual movement from hostility to hospitality.

From Illusion to Prayer

The third movement Nouwen described is the movement from illusion to prayer. We humans have eternity stamped in our hearts. But this desire for immortality and transcendent meaning can be destroyed by the mundane; then it becomes an illusion, rather than reality. The illusion whispers, _Things will always be as they are. I can somehow stop the clock and enter eternity unaffected by age or death or the consequence of choice._ Tragedy, illness, death, or financial problems unmask the illusion and remind us of the fragile and transitory nature of life.

One of the cruelest lies associated with this illusion is the belief that we can pass up an opportunity to express love to those we care about because there is always tomorrow. But things will _not_ always be as they are today. People die. Opportunities for heartfelt conversation are lost. Discovery calls us to live in truth and reality, making the most of the time we are allotted on earth.

Communion is difficult because in connecting with others we must give up some of our cherished notions, preconceived ideas, prejudices, and old ways of looking at things. We cannot always be right. Because we are uncomfortable with the strong emotions that often accompany intimacy, we may develop a lifestyle that leaves little room for genuine fellowship. We must resist the tendency to alienate ourselves from everyone, making it impossible to enjoy love, warmth, and intimacy.

Such isolation is often rationalized by the need to complete certain tasks associated with our work or the upkeep of our homes. Or we pull back to protect ourselves from the potential others have to hurt us. But isolation is always a symptom of deeper spiritual problems; our hearts have been blocked to communion by pain. Once we have released that pain, we are ready to consider deep communion as a part of our spiritual discovery.

Communion with Others

True spirituality moves beyond self-actualization to the consideration of others. In other words, the acid test of communion with God and with the self is the formation of loving community. Take David and Jonathan in the Old Testament, for instance. It is said they loved each other so much their souls cleaved to each other. What a friendship!

The Bible says, "Two are better than one, because they have a good reward for their labor. For if they fall, one will lift up his companion. But woe to him who is alone when he falls, for he has no one to help him up."[13]

Besides reward and consolation, there is also strength in working together. Breaking one stick is easy. Breaking a number of sticks bound together is much more difficult.

Before He started His earthly ministry, Jesus chose twelve men to share that work. Twelve disciples. And in that twelve, He chose Peter, James, and John as His closest friends. A small confidential group. And of that group, one was Jesus' special friend. From the cross Jesus asked that friend, John, "the disciple He loved," to care for His mother. It is natural to have some relationships that are deeper than others. Our deepest sense of communion will be reserved for a precious few.

True spirituality leads to intimate relationships and the development of community—not to withdrawal from society. The Last Supper, during which Holy Communion was initiated, is the call for communion and community. As we partake of the body and blood of Christ, we share intimately in His sufferings while at the same time we commit ourselves more deeply to each other in obedience to seeing God's will done on earth.

Prayer leads us to communion with others.

And this communion leads us to become involved in each other's lives. Unfortunately, however, this sometimes means we tend to rush in and give advice to our friends. And because some people go to prayer groups and self-help groups to get other people to tell them what to do, a strong personality in the group can end up taking away the decision-making ability of the weaker members. This person takes away the weaker members' authority cards. Other destructive communities can also take away people's ability to face their issues, so they come away almost crippled emotionally.

Instead, true community focuses on people developing a relationship with other people—fellowship with each other—rather than just answering a particular need. The key thing is to clarify what the person's need really is through prayer and talking and then allow the person to come to a realization of the answer himself. In true community people are challenged to look at what they really want by opening themselves to prayer. We have a sacred trust to help people clarify their needs and what they want.

On the other hand, once we clarify people's needs

through prayer we are called to help them if they really need help. I often tell the parable of Pudgy, a little Bahamian fish, who loved swimming too close to the beach.

One day Pudgy swam so close to the shore, the waves pushed him up on the beach and stranded him there.

Now a fish out of water is in trouble!

Pudgy flapped his fins desperately to get back into the sea, but to no avail. A few times the tide came within inches of him, then washed back out to sea without carrying him on its back.

Then a man from the Bahamas Independence Society came by and spotted Pudgy. "Oh, little fish," he called out, "you're beached!"

"Yes, and I am getting thirsty. Please put me back in the water or I'll die."

"That's an interesting proposition, little fish. I'm on the way to a committee meeting in which we will discuss how people and fishes can help themselves. You just give a good kick and you'll get back into the water. You can do it by yourself," he said.

Pudgy got weaker and weaker as the Bahamian sun became higher in the sky.

Finally he gave one more push, but couldn't make it. The little fish died on the shore. In the late afternoon the tide rose and took him out to sea.

After his meeting the man from the Bahamas Independence Society came back to the spot and noticed that Pudgy was gone. "Oh, I knew that fish could do it. And he did it all by himself!"

Pudgy is often our heart, our child, our spouse, or our friend, calling out for help. Unfortunately we can be like that man from the Bahamas Independence Society when we or someone we know is hurting. Yet at a certain point in the relationship, action is demanded or the beached one dies. After the clarification, after the listening and the loving, we have to do what we have to do. True community clarifies the time for action.

If we fail to respond, one day the cries for help will stop; the heart will close in on itself and become detached. One woman who heard the Pudgy parable came to the clinic and said, "I am beached and I've come to get some help."

Initial attempts at communion may be characterized by fits and starts. But the sense of belonging and fulfillment associated with healthy community life are worth the effort. And considering the rates of divorce, teenage suicide, and depression, modern society is in deep need of community. What a challenge for the church! This practical, openness of heart toward others is what our world needs more of!

Communion with Creation

Communing with nature is a new experience for me, but when I returned to the Bahamas, I became enraptured by the beauty and poetry of the islands. I started writing this chapter sitting in front of the beautiful, aquamarine colors of the Bahamian sea. At dawn, the waters are dark and somber-looking. But then the sun comes out—and what a change! How splendid to watch the colors of the water dazzle in the sunlight. What a lesson.

Just as the sunlight brings out the beauty of the sea, the love of God shines into the pained, dull spaces of our lives, giving hope and meaning and joy.

I have watched the sea for many hours, but the most disturbing spectacle occurred one day in October, 1991, when a series of tidal waves rushed over the shore. Huge waves crashed fiercely against the sea walls, picking up large boulders as if they were just pebbles. What terrifying power! My heart jumped with fear and awe as I drove along the beach road as quickly as I dared. A huge wave attacked my car, knocking me from side to side. After that I came to respect the sea, and I am beginning to understand why it has been said that those who go down to the sea know the mysteries of God. The thunder of the waves broadcasts the mighty power of the Creator who designed it.

As I continued writing this chapter I went to Kenya on safari. The natural jungle of the Serengeti plain, with its wide-open spaces caressed by the gentle sunshine, warmed my heart. And the animals! I watched the striped zebras prancing around, the massive elephants standing colossally on the plain, the prehistoric hippopotami bathing in a natural pool made by the river, the powerful lions resting after their kill and feast—and I was humbled. Because I have opened my heart to love I can appreciate this beauty as never before.

I find myself in awe with a sense of majesty, recognizing there is a Creator who designed such magnificence. The love of God not only draws us to Him in worship, giving meaning to our personal lives and enhancing our relationships with each other, it inspires in us a sense of responsibility to be better stewards of His beautiful creation. The conservation of nature, the prevention of the pollution of the seas and waterways, along with the maintenance of a clean and healthy environment, is a task that requires our best talents, deep patience, and untiring commitment.

Whether you have the sky, the sea, the mountains, the plains, or a rose to enjoy, God still walks in the gardens of our world. All creation proclaims the wonder of God. Our fellowship with Him and others is often rekindled when we enjoy His handiwork.

This sense of awe at God's universe was something I wanted to share with my son, David, when we sailed off from shore on our ill-fated voyage to Rose Island. And the communion we shared on that memorable journey will always evoke pleasant thoughts of togetherness. Just the sight of an anchor is all it takes to remind us of our own inside joke!

How About You?

Here is an excellent way to consider the role of communion in your own life. Plan a special dinner date with your closest friend. Before you meet together, consider the following experiences.

A Journal of Community

Note a time of close communion with God:

_____

_____

_____

Note a time when you felt especially at ease with yourself:

That time for me is always when I'm enjoying the beauty of the Bahamian sea, so I walk along the seashore many days to give me the peace and refreshment I need. How about you!

_____

_____

_____

Do you consciously set aside time for this type of communion so you can experience the peace you need?

Note a time of meaningful fellowship with a friend:

_____

_____

_____

What factors contribute to your sense of oneness with another?

_____

_____

_____

Did the other person in your story feel as touched by the moment as you were? ☐ Yes ☐ No

If yes, why do you think this moment spoke to both of you?

_____

_____

_____

Note a time when you felt a sense of belonging in a community.

I remember an experience during the seventies in Cambridge, Massachusetts, which was the scene of many different types of communities. I found great support and solace in one of them, the Ware Street Community, a Christian community led by Bob and Barbara Ludwig. This couple opened their two-story house as a residence for transient students and as a center for Bible study and fellowship for any student who desired to attend. Being away from my island home, I was pleased to have a place for meals, conversation, and friendship.

When did you feel a particular sense of community?

_____

_____

_____

What factors contributed to your sense of belonging to a community in this situation?

The time I spent as part of the Ware Street community was a dark night of my soul, a time when my studies at Harvard were forcing me to try to understand my faith in light of the science of psychiatry. The Ludwigs and my friends did not try to solve my problem for me. Instead they responded with fellowship and love and understanding. Sometimes that meant we would read a book together or pray together, other times it meant playing tennis at 7:00 in the morning or jogging together. Love and understanding contributed to my sense of belonging in the Ware Street Community.

What contributed to your sense of belonging in the community you experienced?

_____

_____

_____

Note a time of special communion with nature:

_____

_____

_____

What factors contributed to your sense of communion with nature?

_____

_____

_____

Finally, note a time of bonding or unity during a meal with someone:

In my life a meal is often a physical or material represen-tation of Christ's communion with us. So often in the Ba-hamas we would invite friends to dinner at 8:00 P.M. and still be sitting there at 1:00 A.M., sharing stories and expe-riences.

Describe a time when you experienced a time of bonding during a meal with someone:

_____

_____

_____

What factors contributed to your sense of bonding during this meal?

_____

_____

_____

As you discuss these moments with a friend, have him or her help you look for patterns in the moments you recall.

Communion with God, the common Father of human-kind, allows us to be in touch with the brother and sister-hood of all humankind, which led me to reach out to others in a daring way.

In Knowles House, our drug clinic in the Bahamas, I be-gan to notice an increasing number of patients coming in with cocaine addiction. I felt an ethical responsibility to do something to challenge this new rise of addiction stem-ming from the new drug form, crack-cocaine. Because I wasn't sure what to do, I kept quiet for a number of months.

Then I received a letter from a thirteen-year-old girl. She described how she had gotten high on a special kind of cocaine. The pusher who had introduced her to the drug asked her to turn over her mother's jewelry. She did that.

Then he asked for her mother's china. And she gave him that.

Now he was asking for her body.

She had heard about me, and in desperation wrote the letter, not knowing what else to do.

In my broadened awareness of communion, that little girl was not just one little girl. She was my sister. She was my daughter. She was one of us. And that is when I started the public campaign against cocaine in the Bahamas, which led to the development of a task force against drugs, a lot of research, and eventual control of the addiction epidemic. A heart connection with one poor child changed my homeland. A heart connection with one person can change your life and your world too.

❧8❧

A Spirit of Supernatural Power: Commitment Despite Resistance

My family and I were visiting Cambridge, Massachusetts, when the call came. Gisela, my brother Ted's wife, would never interrupt a vacation unless it was very, very important. The moment I heard her trembling voice I knew something was terribly wrong.

"Fern and her husband have been found dead in their Philadelphia apartment," she told me between sobs. Fern was my niece, the daughter of my elder brother, Ed.

My heart sank as I recalled Fern's visit earlier that year and her delight at being Bradley's wife and the mother of a new baby girl, Lisa. Fern had delicate features and long black hair that hung freely. She was very gentle, polite, and soft-spoken. Like her father (my brother Ed, who was pastor of the Abundant Life Bible Chapel in the Bahamas), she had a deep commitment to the Lord. How could harm come to such a good person?

When I could speak again I asked for details. "How? Why? Who?"

Gisela knew little.

Neither Gisela nor I could find many words to say; I finally broke the painful silence. "Thank you for letting us know. I'll go to Philadelphia as soon as I can."

I hung up the phone and slumped back on the bed. The shock and pain were suffocating. My wife, Vicki, came immediately to see what was the matter. As I told her what Gisela had said we sat in numb silence. The big question was, How should we tell our two children? The protective part of me wanted to hide death from my kids, even though death and evil are part of real life.

We called the children in, shared the news, and held each other. In one sense nothing could have prepared us for the darkness of that hour, yet in another way the concepts in this chapter were the invisible truths that held my shattered heart together during that tragic time.

We all face resistance in the form of disease, death, and suffering, and much of it is out of our control, which makes it so much more painful.

Resistance Is Real for Everyone

Some writers and speakers make light of life. But the "believe-in-God-and-everything-will-work-out-fine" smoke screen can only hide the real world for so long before the truth breaks through. Resistance is real. And normal.

Raw evil exists in our fallen world, and those who seek to discover the wonderful depths of God's love will not be exempt from experiencing this evil. In a deep sense much of life is suffering because:

All life is change.

All change is loss.

All loss is pain.

Christ refused to shield even Himself. At the Last Supper, when the Lord was sharing intimately with His disciples, Judas sat at the table, planning to betray Him.

Suffering. Anguish. Murder of the innocent. History tells us it has happened before. Whenever you decide to live a life of spiritual discovery you will encounter resistance.

Types of Resistance

You may encounter several types of resistance during your life. Let's look at four of the most common types: resistance from our own emotions, resistance from spiritual forces of evil, resistance from our own bad habits and negative thinking patterns, and resistance from our own family and friends.

Resistance from Our Own Emotions

First, resistance can come from our own emotions—our own doubts and fears—as a result of the hurt in our lives. When I arrived in Philadelphia I went immediately to the home of Fern's father-in-law, where my family had gathered. It was so hard to see Fern's father, my brother Ed, who had flown to the States from the Bahamas. He had served God faithfully all his life, first as a missionary on the family islands, then as a pastor in the Bahamas. Now this.

Ed was broken. We looked at each other and then sat together quietly. Fern's mother was also overwhelmed, as were Bradley's mother and father. There are no words for the agony of the four parents in that room.

During the time at the house, people began to fill me in on what happened. Details were scarce, but what _was_ known made a nightmarish story. Fern and Bradley had been at home when some people knocked at their door. When they opened the door, the intruders rushed in and apparently demanded money. Bradley was taken down to the basement and killed. For whatever reason, Fern was taken upstairs, where she was murdered in the bathroom. Their eight-month-old baby, Lisa, was left alive. The police found the baby unharmed, lying beside her mother's dead body.

Questions assaulted all of us. My brother knew the couple's house had been broken into before. In fact they had installed an intricate burglar-alarm system to protect themselves. Ed had felt this system was an answer to his prayers for their safety.

That night, after I had heard the story, it was hard to sleep. I felt alone. Scared. Empty. My mind swirled with unanswered questions. As Fern was dying, did she think of her island home? Her family? What were those final moments like? I wondered what impact this would have on her tiny baby and what Lisa's life would be like. We loved her so much!

There will always be times when doubts and fears come to mind. Discovery is a commitment to the reality of life, which allows us to acknowledge our emotions to God and ourselves in a direct manner. No pretending. No hiding. No berating ourselves because of honest emotions. We simply tell God how we feel in our confusion and hurt, asking Him to reassure and comfort us. Then, with our hearts laid open before Him, we can approach the Bible with eyes to see and ears to hear.

Whenever our safety and security are shattered, we will always feel the emotion of fear. Fern was so gentle and harmless that the thought of her being murdered ripped through our family. For a long time after that my little son, David, would come to me whenever I had to travel to America from the Bahamas. He would look at me with raw fear in his eyes and say, "Daddy, are you going to get murdered like Fern?"

The fear in the child's eyes was also felt in the father's

heart, although I would never admit it. Fear became a resistance for all of us. The tragedy was such a powerful shock it left us worried about one another's safety. In the Bahamas, where I worked at fighting drugs, there was the risk of dangerous situations, volatile addicts, and their connections. As a family we had to spend time talking and praying about the fear. I felt a sense of calling and vocation about my work, and somehow it was easy work for me to do because I knew God wanted me to do it. His presence was with me. There was resistance to my efforts—difficult times, frustrations, and threats on my life— but they didn't upset my heart, which was centered in Christ.

Resistance can also occur when powerful feelings of anger, bitterness, guilt, and discouragement give rise to voices of shame from our past:

- *You are not good enough.*
- *You are a failure.*
- *Life never goes your way.*
- *You can't get ahead.*
- *Nobody cares about you.*
- *Why bother? You'll never succeed anyway.*

How powerful these voices are, discouraging the strongest saints as they try to be missionaries to their own hearts.

Guilt feelings are particularly powerful in our lives, especially in individuals who have gone through a recovery process. Often there is a gap between what they expect of themselves and their actual level of performance in times of trouble. Guilt when one relapses or fails to live up to one's ideal adds unnecessary extra burdens to an already stressful ordeal. But true guilt can be cleansed from the conscience in a matter of moments through repentance and prayers of confession.

False guilt is a psychological phenomenon that must be countered by truth. Our hypersensitive consciences stand ready to accuse us at the least sign of anticipated, exaggerated, or actual relapse into wrongdoing. This creates such rigidity that we often topple under the sheer weight of unrealistic expectations. False guilt leaves us weary and depressed because at every point of resistance we assume too much responsibility for others and for circumstances—we automatically assume we are at fault.

The antidote to these powerful resistances is a childlike, trusting faith in God's love. Simple faith allows us to walk in grace, rather than in our own strength. Grace counteracts fear because even if there is a failure or relapse, forgiveness is available. Thus, one gets back up immediately and continues the pilgrimage into discovery.

Resistance from Spiritual Forces of Evil

In the Bible we are told to expect resistance from spiritual forces of evil. Resistance can also come from evil persons around us.

Later, we learned that my niece and her husband were killed by a man who had a criminal record. The man and a friend had approached the couple as they returned from church that night, then forced themselves in the house and attacked them.

In Chapter 3 I discussed the connection between hurt and anger, and bitterness. If anger is stuffed or repressed it becomes organized within the heart, producing bitterness and hatred. At such times the inner core of the person becomes fertile ground for the demonic.

Repressed anger eats away at the person and simultaneously seeks the destruction of others. At such times close family members can hurt each other, churches may split, and even lovers may destroy one another. How else can we explain a mother hiring a contract killer to shoot her son-in-law? A teacher conspiring with a student lover to kill her husband? Or a mother seeking to have her neighbor killed to prevent the neighbor's daughter from winning the cheerleading competition over her daughter?

In working with scores of persons seeking to move into a deeper understanding of themselves, I also see a strong common experience of spiritual frustration, a lack of meaning, the inability to pray or meditate, or extreme busyness, which makes reflection difficult. The end result is frustration and a restlessness of the heart, which leads to confusion or depression.

In the days following the funeral, my brother's eyes were full of hurt. I will never forget the question Ed asked me in his darkest moment: "Where were the hosts of heaven? Where were the guardian angels?"

Those words pierced me. I looked at him, swallowed hard, and said nothing. What could I say? . . . What could I say?

Only a partial answer could be seen through our tear-blurred eyes. Where *were* the guardian angels? They were escorting Fern and Bradley into the presence of God. And they were bending over the baby. A defenseless soul survived—perhaps on the strength of her parents' anguished prayers on her behalf in the final moments. A loving God protected little Lisa. The same loving God took two of His children home. We don't understand why.

But my brother and I did understand that the openness to talk about our true hurts and questions was healthy. We were not challenging God or criticizing the way He ran the world; we were simply pouring out our hearts before Him as He encourages us to do. We needed His help to cope with the grieving process. We needed each other.

There may have been times when you have believed, as I have, that dark powers were at work in a particular person's life, bringing pain and heartache. We know very few details of Judas Iscariot's life. Although Judas was the human means of resistance at the Last Supper, the Scripture makes it clear that another dimension of the resistance was demonic: "The devil . . . put into the heart of Judas Iscariot, . . . to betray Him."[1] Even so, Jesus did not interrupt His mission, and God's will ultimately prevailed. The feast goes marching on!

The apostle Paul reminds us that our battle is not "against flesh and blood, but against principalities, against powers, against the rulers of the darkness of this age, against spiritual hosts of wickedness in the heavenly places"[2] Because the battle is spiritual, the weapons of our warfare must also be spiritual:

- The sword of the Spirit (the Word of God)
- The breastplate of righteousness (the righteousness of obedience to Christ)
- The helmet of salvation (the sure knowledge of God's saving love)
- The shoes of the good news of peace (the forgiveness and reconciliation we have received because of Christ's death in our place)

Reliance on these great spiritual truths must be buttressed by continual prayer as we constantly look to God's strength rather than our own. "He who is in you is greater than [the evil one] who is in the world."[3]

Resistance from Our Own Bad Habits and Negative Thinking Patterns

Change is not easy. Compulsions and addictions tag along on our journeys of life unless we actively break away from them.

Consider the habit of discouragement. Perhaps when things went wrong in the past we gave in to feelings of helplessness, hopelessness, and unworthiness—a common threesome. Rather than follow our inner convictions to do things differently, we may bow codependently to the dictates of the circumstances or people around us. _He won't like me if I do this_, or _They will think I am stupid_, or _I may fail and people will laugh at me_, or _I can't make it, I am too weak._

On other occasions we may resist our own progress with "if-only" arguments: _If only I had a better education_, or _If only I had a better marriage_, or _If I had a better job_, or _If I had more time_, or _If my family understood_, or _If my church were more supportive._

All these are in fact internal resistances preventing us from achieving our true potential. As C. S. Lewis wisely said in his essay, "A Weight of Glory," "The only people who achieve much are those who want knowledge so badly that they seek it while conditions are still unfavorable. Favorable conditions never come."

Resistance from Family and Friends

Perhaps the most powerful external resistance to growth is the power of the social environment. Saul, when asked why he had refused to obey God's command to destroy the Amalekites, replied, "I feared the people [more than I feared God] and obeyed their voice."[4]

Conformity is so powerful that many of us throw away our best efforts in order to please the crowd or gain social acceptance. People in recovery develop a fear of rejection by the surrounding society. Yet the crowd is fickle. After all, the crowd called for the crucifixion of Jesus.

The goal cannot be to win acceptance from others, but rather to live true to our convictions and to our God.

Oppressive modern influences to achieve, compete, and excel are associated with extreme busyness and stress. Unless persons in discovery learn to pace themselves, they could lose perspective and find themselves overwhelmed with no time for their inner life.

The heart is the battleground of life, where our true allegiances will be decided. Loyalty to God liberates us from the tyranny of conformity because "if God is for us, who can be against us?"[5]

Resistance to personal growth and change often comes from those in our own family or circle of friends. Judas was Jesus' disciple, His friend. He had spent three years with Jesus and was the trusted accountant and steward of the community's resources.

We know few details of Judas' life. Yet we might surmise that he suffered some unresolved hurt earlier in life that led him to repress his authentic self. For whatever reason, his false self—the part of him that wanted approval and desired power—gave in to the repressed hurt and anger that controlled his life. As a result, a demonic spirit grew in his heart and finally led him to betray the Lord.

I can see Christ looking at Judas and saying to him, "Judas, you don't need those thirty pieces of silver. You are too dependent on money and popularity. Why are you doing this? Judas, you are a real person, and I love you. Don't you understand, Judas? I am God. I am not on trial, Judas. *You* are. I love you, Judas. Change your mind."

But oh, the power of the false self. Judas did not allow His love to break through to his heart.

We too may be betrayed or discouraged by our family or friends. It is a known phenomenon that a prophet is not accepted in his own home. It is extremely difficult for those familiar with us to let go of their past perceptions and prejudices of us. A casual look of disdain, a sarcastic remark, or a belittling comment can throw the strongest person back on the road to self-doubt and lack of confidence.

We must realize that growth in the individual always

sends vibrations of challenge to those in our closest circle.

Secure persons will encourage growth in another, while less secure friends or relatives become threatened and withdraw, criticizing and finding fault. The road to discovery means saying good-bye to the security of home, the old influences, empty traditions, harmful patterns of relating, family jinxes. Only if we are willing to say good-bye to the old can we say hello to the new community of persons within or outside our family who choose to transcend the daily march of mediocrity to reach for the stars.

This does not mean an automatic rejection of family. Rather, it is a warning that family members know about our emotional buttons and they are very effective in pushing them at the wrong time. And we are more vulnerable to the comments of those who are near and dear to us. As one insightful college student remarked, "The time to tell my father about a problem is after I've successfully solved it!"

Peer pressure from friends and family is a very common resistance. The decision to grow to discover one's potential means that a person may have to say good-bye to friends or acquaintances connected to his or her previous life. Many times former peers become jealous and feel threatened when one of their group moves beyond them.

After a year of successful treatment in a rehabilitation program, a young man returned home to the community where he had become addicted to crack-cocaine. The day he came home, his "friends" threw a two-hundred-dollar crack-cocaine rock on his porch. He said, "Dr. Allen, I looked at the rock and wanted to just leave it. Then I picked it up and tried to throw it back to them. But it just would not leave my hand. So I hit up on it! And the addiction started all over again."

Perhaps the hardest thing about moving into discovery is the realization that you may have to stand alone . . . sometimes encountering the rejection of those close to you. The truth is that people will fail us. Even in the church some of our closest associates will disagree or speak against us. It is natural to feel hurt and angry and to want revenge when this happens. But the challenge of our faith is to firmly push on with our convictions in an attitude of love and compassion.

How to Face Resistance

How you meet mild or severe resistance will change your heart—for good or for evil. Often it is not only a traumatic event that works against you, but also it is your own response to the situation. In this section we'll look at some ways you can face resistance and move on in your journey toward discovery.

Realize Personal Growth Happens in Spite of Resistance

You may want to run away. Your heart may try to hide or escape, but resistance must be met as an unavoidable pit on the path of discovery. Trials and tribulations do not have to stop the process of spiritual growth. Rather, these unwelcome storms in life can help us clarify our values and gain a clearer view of God's love.

In the very midst of the heartrending news of the double murders of my niece and her husband, the powerful truth was that God was still with our family. During those dark days these words were medicine to my troubled heart:

Who shall separate us from the love of Christ? Shall tribulation, or distress, or persecution, or famine, or nakedness, or peril, or sword? . . . Yet in all these things we are more than conquerors through Him who loved us. For I am persuaded that neither death nor life, nor angels nor principalities nor powers, nor things present nor things to come, nor height nor depth, nor any other created thing, shall be able to separate us from the love of God which is in Christ Jesus our Lord.[6]

Be Open to Help from God and Others

We need to share our burdens with one another. It was important for my brother and me to talk to one another, and not allow our pain to wall us off. We may all feel the urge to withdraw from time to time, but it is important that we do not isolate ourselves in the face of resistance. There really is strength in numbers.

Even when we can't understand, we know God is still on His throne. When we can't put our feelings into words, we can take comfort in knowing God hears the groans of those who love Him. And just as the destructive intentions and act of Judas did not deter the purpose of Christ's life, the violence of broken, detached men from the Philadelphia ghetto could not overrule God's plan for us. I reminded myself, *Those men acted out of their own hurt trail. Pity them. Pray for them. But don't doubt God because of them!*

The Support of Community. When you face resistance, it is also extremely helpful to meet with other believers. Meaningful fellowship and support from others who believe as you do provide a steady stream of comfort and encouragement. This might be a church, a small Bible study, or a discovery group—or all three—where you can openly express yourself without fear of rejection or doctrinal attack. Meaningful fellowship is more than just moving along the group's party line; it is the freedom to explore and resolve your true emotions and questions. When I felt doubts and fears after the murders, my friends provided affirmation of my vocation and many prayers on my behalf.

My friends were realists in the sense that they never tried to pretend God had promised me a life that would always be smooth sailing. Many persons have turned from the journey of discovery because they were led to believe they would not encounter resistance and suffering in their new life. Or they had not been instructed how to face that resistance in faith.

Look at the Broad Perspective

The final suggestion for those facing resistance is to look at the wider picture of what God is doing in the world, rather than just focusing on the problem at hand. God is sovereign, and even when we do not understand His ways, we can be assured that "all things work together for good to those who love God, to those who are the called according to His purpose."[7]

I realized this the day of Fern and Bradley's funeral. I dreaded attending that service, especially after I visited the church that morning and saw those two young, handsome persons lying in their coffins. To me it was death in the raw.

Later, as I dressed automatically for the funeral I felt myself not wanting to go on one hand, and on the other, wanting to attend to show my love for Fern and my support for my brother Ed and his wife.

Once I got to the church, a lot of my ambivalence seemed to die away. I sat down as the organ was playing, "Face to face, with Christ my Saviour," a beautiful old song my mother used to sing. As I listened, somehow my heart was eased.

I have always believed one of the real gifts of the presence of God's spirit is the absence of fear. That's why Paul's words of encouragement in 2 Timothy have always been important to me: "For God has not given us a spirit of fear, but of power and of love and of a sound mind."[8]

My fear and ambivalence moved away, and I began to think about what these two lives represented. I spoke to the mourners gathered together, sharing some of my thoughts. "Fern was always quiet and deeply committed to her faith in Christ," I said. "As I recall her memory, I think of her as a beautiful flower. It is sad that the flower was picked at a very early age . . . but she bloomed and blossomed by bringing encouragement and love to those who knew her. Many times I was encouraged just by being around her quiet spirit. And Bradley was always so full of life. My last memory of him is jogging with him in Connecticut. His speed and stride were twice mine. He finished the run fifteen minutes before I did! They were two vibrant, fun people who enjoyed being alive. Life is so transitory. Yet their faith—the meaning of their lives—lives on."

My brother also spoke. He talked about Fern as a little girl who seemed to be very devoted to the Lord, as a young adult who went to Houghton College in New York for premedical studies, as the bride who gave up her desire to be a doctor to marry Bradley, and as the loving mother of baby Lisa. "This is the biggest trial of my life," he said. "It is a trial of my faith."

Everyone was moved by his openness. He ended his statements by saying, "I choose to trust in God."

What struck me was that in the midst of his pain, in the midst of his anger, fear, and hurt, he was making a statement of faith. Looking at the pure facts, feeling the crushing emotions, his heart surely cried out *Where was God?* Yet his mind and emotions were submitted to His will. Even though he didn't understand, he chose to believe in God.

He was affirming that, in spite of the pain, all was well with his soul. And even though all was well with his soul there were still tears in his eyes!

Yet darker days lay ahead of him. Once he returned to the Bahamas to serve his church, he began to question the very existence of God. He knew the evil one was putting those thoughts in his mind, but they wouldn't go away. He told us later that he began a continual "powwow," with God, asking, *What do Your promises really mean? Where was Your army when my daughter needed help? Can I really trust You? Could You be punishing me for something I've done?*

A few weeks after the funeral one of the members of his congregation who was suffering from a brain tumor asked him to visit her in the hospital. Out of duty, he went.

The young girl's face brightened as Ed walked into the room. But when she asked him to pray for her, Ed stood there without speaking. He felt he had no contact with God. God had either abandoned him or he had abandoned God. *If I pray for her, will God listen?* he wondered. *If so, why didn't He hear me before when I asked Him to protect Fern and her husband?* Despite his doubts, my brother started to pray—and then couldn't finish. He abruptly left the room and stood in the passageway outside, feeling depressed. Prayer seemed to be useless.

A few weeks later, after a guest preacher had spoken about Daniel and his trials in the lions' den, a young girl who was a new believer came up to Ed after the service.

"I can't understand it," she said. "You are so godly and caring. You help so many people. I can't understand how God allowed this to happen to your family."

Ed had no answer for her. Instead he said, "You are new in the faith. Let me handle this . . . You don't understand and neither do I, but if it's going to puzzle anyone, let it puzzle me."

After the girl walked away, Ed challenged God as he had at the hospital: *You see, God. You see what You are doing? You are bringing disgrace to Your name. How can I pray for others? How can I counsel them after what has happened?*

Ed believed many people in our island community were

wondering the same thing. He became ashamed to go out as a minister of the gospel.

Then a friend shared with him a verse near the end of Romans 8: "He . . . did not spare His own Son, but delivered Him up for us all."⁹ In the next days Ed realized God wanted to take him further in his ministry, but He couldn't do that until He took him deeper, to appreciate Him, to depend upon Him—to lengthen the cords of his tent (Isa. 54:2).

That was five or six years ago. Ed recently told me, "As painful as those deaths were, my most meaningful ministry has occurred since then. The church has grown. I have been able to complete my academic work" (a master's of theology, followed by an honorary doctorate degree). I have noticed a tremendous depth in his preaching.

Ed did not simply hold his ground in the face of resistance; he has made significant advances in his spiritual journey. I don't understand this and don't want to interpret it, but he has come to a deeper experience of God and a deeper revelation of God's love for him, and this has been manifested in the growth and development of his ministry.

God may operate on a different timetable from the one we prefer, but He makes all things work for good in His time. Do not be surprised by difficult trials that enter your life. Yield them to God just as simply as you do the joys and blessings. We do not have to invite harm or add to our sufferings in our effort to be spiritual, of course, but we should be well rooted in God before the inevitable storms of life hit home.

In discovery there will always be resistance. The challenge is to move forward in spite of it. The goal is to use the resistance as a means to spur us on to even greater depths of discovery.

As I have returned to Nassau over the years, I have had the chance to spend time with my brother and his family and to see Fern's little daughter, Lisa, grow and change as they reared her as their own. It always amazed me that she was such a pleasant and happy child.

Last year I took her for a little ride, and out of the blue this eight-year-old girl said to me, "Uncle David, my mommy and daddy are not my real mommy and daddy, you know." The way she phrased the remark caught me off guard; apparently she had heard the tragic story and was sorting things through. "Lisa, what do you mean?"

She went on, "Well, people killed my mommy and daddy."

We rode for a while in silence. Then came the question that tore at my heart. She asked me, "Uncle David, why did they kill my mommy and daddy?"

I put my arm around her as I prayed silently, *Lord, I don't understand this child's heart, but I can feel the pain tearing my own heart so I can imagine what her little heart must feel. In Your grace put Your arms around her and hold her to Yourself, so as she grows she may grow with Your love, Your protection, and Your guidance. Even though I can't answer her question or protect her from this horrible hurt and pain, I trust You, the God of all comfort, to comfort her. Help me to be a special support to Lisa right now. . . . Let my love help carry her.*

After this prayer I had a sense that God's presence would somehow take charge. And it did.

In moments such as these I have found God's adequacy sufficient whenever I am desperately inadequate. This is the discovery process, which allows our hearts to embrace reality and achieve serenity, even when we don't understand and life is not easy.

Resistance is real, but it is not eternal. In the end love wins.

9

A Spirit of Divestiture: Humility

The wealthy and cultured Charles M. de Lambert III was dubbed "Sir Lambert" by his therapy group. A tall, tanned man with jet-black hair and expensive gold jewelry, he came to group sessions to dispense help, not to receive it.

Lambert had sold his businesses and, it seemed, had quite a bit of money. He had known me for several years, and believed he now had enough time to do a little work on himself, polishing up his image. Personally, I think he wanted to impress the group and me with just how "together" he was. A new Christian, he felt his wealth and newfound faith put him on top of the world—and he wanted to tell everyone else how to climb up beside him!

Sir Lambert was constantly postulating on whatever topic we were discussing, and to the group's credit, everyone endured him with patience the first few weeks—until they finally got fed up with his arrogant "do-this-and-do-that" sermonettes. After that, they began making sport of Sir Lambert behind his back, mock-saluting and such when he went past.

Sir Lambert was surprised that group members started avoiding him. It got so bad that when he began to speak their body language and the roll of their eyes said quite visibly, *Oh, no. Not again.*

Then one afternoon he entered the room briskly in his tailored slacks and designer shirt, ready to set the group members' lives straight. Fifteen minutes later he told them they needed to get their lives together as he had, and everything would be fine.

Lanna, an educated, soft-spoken woman, protested, "I'm sorry, but all your talk does nothing for me."

Charles M. de Lambert III was a man accustomed to being listened to by his subordinates (primarily because he owned the company, so who could ignore him?), and the thought that he had nothing of value to say was completely foreign to him. "What do you mean?" he asked. "I know I can help you if you come to Christ the way I did."

"You cannot help me. If anything, your speeches put me off," the woman said candidly. "You say you have arrived, but I get the impression you still have a lot to learn."

When Lanna said that, the whole group began to chime in:

"We've really been finding you very difficult. You preach at us without sharing with us."

"We don't want what you've got. That's not how we want to live."

"You play like you have it together, but we don't believe you have it together at all. We believe that down deep you're really hurting. And with your arrogance you are defending against the hurt in your own heart."

I watched Sir Lambert's stiff upper body slump deep into his chair so that his chin nearly touched his gold tie clip. Then he sat straight up again and shot back, "But you guys don't understand me!"

The group members responded that they had listened to

him for three weeks as he had gone on and on about what he'd done and what he'd achieved. "You knock us over the head with your new faith, but it sounds very empty."

Sir Lambert came to the next session a changed man. Shortly after the session began he addressed the group, "Last week you really shook me up. I thought I was really in charge of my life and knew a lot of the answers. But you didn't buy it, and as I considered your remarks later neither did I."

He went on to share that Lanna, the first woman to express her thoughts, had mentioned the very same problems he had heard from someone else—his wife. She had been telling him for weeks that she found it very difficult to relate to him. In fact, he wondered if Lanna had talked to his wife!

"It looks like I need to take another look at my life," the businessman continued. "You were right. It's not all together. I am hurting."

From that moment on the humble Sir Lambert became an important member of the group as he related his honest pain and viewpoint from humility, not arrogance.

Who Is the Greatest?

Everyone who smiled at the story of this man's reckless ego can admit there is a Sir Lambert side to all of us. Sometimes others have to notice our lack of humility before we become aware of it ourselves.

Humility and the search for the heart are intertwined. Sometimes, although we set out to minister to others in the power of God, dependent upon His grace, we somehow ease into a Sir Lambert-style attitude when we assume that everything rests upon us, believing:

We are God's gift to needy people.

We have to know everything.

We have to be everything.

We have to be totally available.

Pride and perfectionism become our taskmasters, and self-righteousness soon follows. Then the ends we wanted to achieve somehow get twisted to become the means to our own advancement, satisfaction, and image as "good" people. Without humility, we fall away from the simplicity of trusting God to help us and others.

By contrast, author Richard Foster describes Christ's humility and servanthood this way:

> When Jesus gathered His disciples for the Last Supper they were having trouble over who was the greatest. This was no new issue for them. . . . Whenever there is trouble over who is the greatest there is trouble over who is the least. That is the crux of the matter for us, isn't it? Most of us know we will never be the greatest; just don't let us be the least.
>
> Gathered at the Passover feast the disciples were keenly aware that someone needed to wash the others' feet. The problem was that the only people who washed feet were the least. So there they sat, feet caked with dirt. It was such a sore point that they were not even going to talk about it. No one wanted to be considered the least. Then Jesus took a towel and a basin and so redefined greatness.[1]

You may be wondering, as I once did, why it was so obvious that someone had to wash the guests' feet. William Barclay explains this in his commentary on the Gospel of John:

> The roads of Palestine were unsurfaced and uncleaned. In dry weather they were inches deep in dirt and in wet

they were liquid mud. The shoes ordinary people wore were sandals, which were simply soles held on to the foot by a few straps. They gave little protection against the dust or the mud of the roads. For that reason there were always great waterpots at the door of the house, and a servant was there with a ewer [vase-shaped jug] and a towel to wash the soiled feet of the guests as they came in.[2]

There was no servant at the Last Supper. Christ chose that role for Himself. Stripping Himself of His garments, He clothed Himself in the garb of a servant. By doing so He chose to divest Himself of power, making a statement to His followers concerning their arrogant strivings. In essence, He was telling them, "In order to know who I am, you must learn to humble yourselves."

Many of us know the value of true humility, but we're afraid to be humble because humility requires us to be vulnerable and open. The resulting pride often manifests itself in three areas: an undue worship of (and need for) the extraordinary, an illusion of permanence and desire for control, and enslavement to materialism.

Worship of the Extraordinary

When we lack humility we may begin to worship the extraordinary and have disdain for things that are ordinary, small, or mundane. We cry out for the big time. The preacher wants sensational crowds; the businessman wants to strike it rich; the professor rushes to publish more papers. We want more media coverage, a larger office in a better location, extraordinary accomplishment in our chosen field. We come to hate our ordinary marriage, our ordinary home, our ordinary looks, our ordinary life. We hate the thought of being average—although the very meaning of the word ensures that most of us _are_ average.

We bring up our children to expect a great deal from life. TV kids listen to ego slogans such as, "You deserve the best." "Proud to be an American." "Be all that you can be." Their extraordinary expectations may far exceed what normal life can provide on a regular basis. Then they are tempted to seek relief or sensational entertainment or pleasure in drugs, sex, and delinquency. Even adults may fill their hearts with despair over an unrealized dream that is far beyond their capabilities. As a result the dream becomes a noose around our necks rather than a positive, motivating force. I know. Pride, as John told me so long ago in Boston, is one of my weaknesses.

We doctors, perhaps more often than most individuals, can become inflated with our importance because we are often involved in literal life-or-death situations. When I was working hard at fighting the war against the drug epidemic in the Bahamas, balancing my family life, and trying to make my medical practice run smoothly, I was sometimes overwhelmed. The responsibilities were so great, and I was so limited. So exhausted.

I came home one evening, rested my head in my hands, and released it all to God. For several moments I humbly bowed in prayer and remained silent before God. Then I poured out my heart: *Lord, this is Your battle. There's no way I can fight it. I don't have the power. I don't have the expertise. I humbly take all these issues and give them over to You. The treatment programs, the community awareness, the lives that need changing . . . Lord, these are Your responsibilities now, Your battles. I acknowledge that without You I am unable to even love my own family the way I want to.*

In that hushed and holy moment a wonderful Bible verse spoke to my heart:

Come to Me, all you who labor and are heavy laden,
and I will give you rest. Take my yoke upon you and
learn from me, for I am gentle and lowly in heart, and
you will find rest for your souls. For My yoke is easy and
My burden is light.[3]

As I gave everything over to God, the very heavy load of
work and concerns I had been carrying slid off my back. I
rested. I felt a precious freedom—as though I had suddenly
been set free from the weight of the world. This exaggerated metaphor made me laugh as I imagined a global earth
rolling off my shoulders. _What is the weight of the world
doing on your back in the first place, Allen?_ I asked myself. No wonder I felt crushed!

Like a kite lifted by a breeze high in the sky, laughter
rides on our ability to be humble. We are helpless in many
situations, flawed, imperfect, and capable of humorous
blunders. Why not admit it and enjoy a good laugh? When
we refuse to take ourselves too seriously, we discover a new
kindness toward ourselves and others—and a refreshing
lightness in life. When we are humble enough to know for
certain we cannot do everything, we become content to set
about doing something, even a very small thing. And, wonder of wonders, we begin to bring about lasting change!

I always remind myself how God has seemed to seek out
ways to work with the ordinary—a little town of Bethle-
hem, an ordinary young girl named Mary, a little boy with
a plain lunch of bread and fish. When we yield our ordinary
life to God, He makes it count for something of eternal
value. Because God is in it the little becomes great; the ordinary shepherd boy's sling kills the giant Goliath. We need
to start life where we are, as we are. In humility we can
accept who we are and become all God means for us to
be—starting this moment with what we have.

The Illusion of Permanence

Pride also shows up as we cling to the illusion of permanence, the belief that everything will always be the same so that we can always be in charge. Now is all that matters. We try to order the perfect life by making more money, seeking more power, finding perfect relationships, settling down in the best neighborhood. Then things change. An illness or accident or unexpected event destroys the illusion of permanence. Someone else seems to be calling the shots. A boss. Fickle fate. And our feeling of narcissistic entitlement becomes a narcissistic despair.

Remembering the temporal nature of life helps keep us humble and keeps worldly accomplishment and prestige in perspective. "The world is passing away, and the lust of it. . ."[4] James reminded the early Christians, "You do not know what will happen tomorrow. For what is your life? It is even a vapor that appears for a little time and then vanishes away."[5] Thus an eternal perspective allows us to appreciate the temporal without being controlled by it. Our careers, which are temporal, should never be allowed to choke our vocation, which is eternal.

Enslaved by Materialism

Pride is also evident in our need for ownership and materialism. *When I get a beautiful house (or glamorous car or an advanced degree), then I'll be special.* We reduce life to what can be seen and touched, believing our possessions and material gain make us persons. We labor to give our children materialistic security rather than the faith that sustained our fathers. Of course this is vanity. No one knew this better than King Solomon, the wealthiest king of Israel, who had more gold, more livestock, and more wives than any man alive. Despite this, he ends the book of Ecclesiastes with a real downer: "All is vanity."[6]

The Christian faces two major realities—the physical and the spiritual. Our faith calls us to accept the spiritual as the predominant reality and the physical as symbolic. A meal is not just satisfying a biological craving but a witness of God's spiritual provision for us. We need to remember the words of the apostle Paul, "the things which are seen are temporary, but the things which are not seen are eternal."[7] The invisible essentials—love, faith, joy, peace, truth, kindness—need to take precedence over the material world we live in because "one's life does not consist in the abundance of the things he possesses."[8]

Humble hearts recognize that there is more to life than who ends up with the most toys. (We have a colloquialism in the Bahamas for this: "Belly full but soul empty.")

This means we have to take off the heavy clothing of success, education, professionalism; we have to step out of our robes of self-righteousness, denominationalism, and tradition. These heavy garments can block our relationship with God and cause alienation that separates us from each other.

But divestiture—shedding the trappings of power and ego—is easier to discuss than to do. Lanna, the woman who set Sir Lambert straight, was a beautiful young lady who, though educated and sophisticated, had fallen into cocaine. In talking of her dad, who had died, she said, "My father was a great doctor, respected by everyone, but I never knew him as my daddy. He never had time for me. He could never lower himself enough to be real at my level."

How tragic! It is possible to achieve great heights and yet miss touching the persons who need us most. This is only possible if we are able to be real with those close to us.

What do your kids say about you? They may know you as a great doctor, a great minister, a great business person, but do they know you as their daddy or their mommy? Do they know who you really are, your fears and your weaknesses as well as your strengths?

Some people see the lack of humility as the core of social injustice and the rat race to own more and bigger things. Even the ministry has its pecking order and the congregation its class structures.

James, a retired pastor of the first-century church, warned these Christians about the danger of pride:

> My brethren, do not hold the faith of our Lord Jesus Christ, the Lord of glory, with partiality. For if there should come into your assembly a man with gold rings, in fine apparel, and there should also come in a poor man in filthy clothes, and you pay attention to the one wearing the fine clothes and say to him, "You sit here in a good place," and say to the poor man, "You stand there," or, "Sit here at my footstool," have you not shown partiality among yourselves, and become judges with evil thoughts?[9]

James was obviously describing situations he had seen in the early church. Is he also describing your church? Do the choir members see themselves as ever so special? The altar guild? The elders? How are people who are poor or ill or emotionally unstable treated in your church?

James warned the early church members, "If you show partiality, you commit sin, and are convicted by the law as transgressors."[10]

In fact most of the chapters in the book of James speak about pride and the need for humility. Other writers in the Bible echoed this theme. The apostle Peter said:

> Be clothed with humility, for "God resists the proud, but gives grace to the humble." Therefore humble your-

selves under the mighty hand of God, that He may exalt you in due time.[11]

Christ's life embodied the principle of divestiture; He was always clothed in humility. But note that He did not give up His identity, His calling, or His ability to do something significant. The apostle Paul described the humbleness of Christ this way:

> Being in the form of God, [Jesus] did not consider it robbery to be equal with God, but made Himself of no reputation, taking the form of a servant, and coming in the likeness of men. And being found in appearance as a man, He humbled Himself and became obedient to the point of death, even the death of the cross.[12]

An Exercise in Humility

Humility is one of those virtues that happens to us when we aren't trying to achieve it. To strive for a humble heart can be counterproductive. The following exercises, however, may help you evaluate the attitude of your heart and clarify your thoughts about divestiture and humility. As I've mentioned before, it is most helpful to write out your answers.

Describe a time or times when you were humiliated. I wrote:

I remember one occasion that stands out to me. I was involved with a major event, a demonstration, and I had written my speech. I hadn't memorized it because I thought I would just read it. After the demonstration the camera lights were on me, and I started to read my speech. But because the bright lights were interfering with my vision, I couldn't really see the speech to read. And I just made a mumble-bumble of the speech.

Now it's your turn.

_____

_____

_____

How did it feel?

I felt terrible because I had planned this situation and it was a perfect time to stress the points we wanted to make. I felt humiliated and embarrassed because I made a mess of it.

How about you?

_____

_____

_____

Write your own simple definitions for both words.

Humiliation is _____

_____

True humility is _____

_____

With those definitions in mind, what is the difference between humility and humiliation?

My definition of humiliation is a sense of failure, shame, and of losing face. Humility, on the other hand, is being open and having a sense of self-acceptance so you are willing to face the issues of your life. It is not easy to maintain.

Now write your thoughts:

_____

_____

_____

Why do you think you sometimes feel a need to exaggerate your sense of significance?

I realize all of us feel threatened sometimes, and we cover up. Human beings are the only animals that can lie to themselves. Human beings can make white look black, and black seem white. So often, our hearts can make us see things that may not be the reality. And ego replaces humility as the deception takes root.

Now it's your turn for introspection:

_____

_____

_____

How can you become comfortable enough being yourself to resist the need to put on airs?

I think we all have that tendency. But I find it most diffi-cult when I am afraid, when I feel limited or inadequate, and when I feel unaccepted. That is when we need to resist the urge to assert ourselves and exaggerate our strengths. For me, prayer is a great help in working through my feelings until I am comfortable with myself and at ease with others.

What can you do?

_____

_____

_____

In the Bible, fasting is often connected with the idea of humbling oneself before God. Institute a weekly or monthly time of fasting when you reduce meals or eliminate them. Write out an ongoing account of your experiences and thoughts during this time. Fasting is not an end in itself or a way to be a better Christian, but it is an effective way to humble ourselves before God and remember our dependence on Him. During the morning or evening of the fast reflect on the verse "For we brought nothing into this world, and it is certain we can carry nothing out."[13]

As you work through these exercises, remember that humility is not pretending to be less able than we are. It is stepping outside the achievement mind-set entirely, refusing to play superiority-inferiority games. Humble people recognize that education, net worth, skin color, physical appearance, and talents have no real bearing on matters of the heart. The heart is not dressed in any of these things. Just ask Sir Lambert.

10

A Spirit of Inner and Outer Harmony: Simplicity

Suzanne slipped away from the room where her two preschoolers were playing. When she thought of the many tasks on her schedule, she dreaded even getting started, but she pushed a strand of hair off her forehead and entered the bathroom to organize and clean the cabinets. When she opened the cabinet doors she groaned at the sight. The shelves were crammed full. Bottles of vitamin pills, children's cold medicines, old prescriptions, and assorted beauty products were piled on one another, pushed into every nook and cranny.

In a moment of painful clarity and insight she thought: *This cabinet, crammed full of too many things is a picture of my life. Disorder. Confusion. I don't want to live this way. God, help me!*

So, in one of the most unlikely settings, Suzanne moved forward on her spiritual journey of discovery. As she began to empty the cabinet and sort through the mess, Suzanne prayed, *Father, I know You are trying to teach me something. Help me understand.*

Simplicity of Outward Life

Many people are caught up in complex nets of hurts, worries, stresses, and demands. Their energy is waning. Their hearts are burdened. Their interactions and contributions to relationships and vocations suffer. This pervasive sense of being overwhelmed should be our red flag, warning us to concentrate and restrict our lives. Less is more.

Anne Morrow Lindbergh wrote, in her book *Gift from the Sea;*

> I remember again, ironically, that today more of us in America than anywhere else in the world have the luxury of choice between simplicity and complication of life. And for the most part, we, who could choose simplicity, choose complication. War, prison, survival periods, enforce a form of simplicity on man. The monk and the nun choose it of their own free will. But if one accidentally finds it, as I have for a few days, one finds also the serenity it brings.[1]

She goes on to say:

> Simplification of outward life is not enough, it is merely the outside. But I am starting with the outside, I am looking at the outside of my life, the shell. The complete answer is not to be found on the outside in an outward mode of living. This is only a technique; a road to grace. The final answer, I know, is always inside but the outside can give a clue, can help one to find the answer inside. One it seems, like the hermit crab, can change one's shell.[2]

Simplicity means organizing one's life to have the basic requirements—health, food, a home—and a meaningful faith, which provides hope and meaning to life. Simplicity means living life with open hands and realizing you don't really own anything because no matter what you have, you will leave it behind. We must own things loosely.

Simplicity is a childlike approach to life. Jesus told His disciples, "Unless you . . . become as little children, you will by no means enter the kingdom of heaven."[3]

Simplicity means living in such a way that our possessions do not obstruct our eternal view of life. Unfortunately, our schedules and our jobs sometimes become so powerful they destroy our vocation. They become our reason for living. Then we become spiritually poor.

At times all of us ache to do less and have it matter more. Anxiety over responsibility can elevate our stress levels very quickly. Simplicity is a welcome antidote to the mad rush of modern living. But true simplification does not mean merely adjusting one's schedule or ordering one's environment, although those are often necessary changes for our well-being.

Pope John XXIII, who made so many revolutionary changes in the Roman Catholic Church, commented, "The older I grow the more clearly I perceive the dignity and winning beauty of simplicity in thought, conduct, and speech: a desire to simplify all that is complicated and to treat everything with the greatest naturalness and clarity."[4]

A cluttered heart leads to a cluttered schedule; an undivided heart leads to simplicity. When I analyze my own life, I evaluate it in four different areas:

- Simplicity of heart
- Simplicity of actions
- Simplicity of word
- Simplicity of vocation

Examine your life with me as we look at each area.

Simplicity of Heart

Pure devotion and childlike wonder can be crowded out by the complexities of adult life. We have to make room in our hearts for simple truth, love, and spirituality.

Jesus lived with an inner harmony of heart that translated into outward harmony, pure and striking simplicity. After taking off His outer garments and wrapping Himself in a towel, our Lord used a basin of water and a towel to wash the disciples' feet. We see Jesus using the simple objects—water, a basin, and a towel—to express His love and commitment to His disciples. Too often we make relationships so complex we ignore the simple, the ordinary . . . a glass of water, a chat, saying good morning, a telephone call, a letter.

Although it is nice to have exciting, elaborate (and often expensive) vacations and experiences, most of our relationships with other people are found in the simple experiences of everyday life. Thus Saint Augustine wrote, "Do not plan long journeys because whatever you believe in, you have already seen. When a thing is everywhere, the way to find it is not to travel, but to love."[5]

In today's world we run all over the place. But if you live on the beach time slows down. You watch the sea, the sky, and the sand. In 1980, I returned to my home in the Bahamas, a land surrounded by the beautiful aquamarine sea. With its myriad interracial and cultural mixtures, the Caribbean has a way of opening my heart, reminding me that life is found in *living*. Life of the heart is inviting a lonesome tourist into your home for quiet conversation. It is visiting a shack devoid of all the world's goods, and when the poor lady prays you feel like the pauper instead of her. Life of the heart is sitting by the sea and letting it teach you.

In the Bahamas we say, "Ketch you-self. Keep it cool, Mon, keep it cool." We are warning each other, "Don't get all upset, all worried. Don't let your life get out of balance."

Of her retreat to her island, Anne Morrow Lindbergh concluded, "I want first of all, above these other desires, to be at peace with myself. I want a singleness of eye, a purity of intension, a central core to my life that will enable me to carry out these obligations and activities as well as I can."[6]

Simple things: The commitment to do what you said you would do. The commitment to refuse to live beyond your means emotionally or financially. The commitment to consider another's interests ahead of your own. These are the building blocks of character and peace of mind that are within reach for every individual.

Simplicity is freedom; duplicity is bondage. Simplicity brings joy and balance; duplicity brings anxiety and fear. Some people equate simplicity with the olden days, and in these people's minds "the olden days" means regression. But the simplicity I speak of has nothing to do with a retreat to primitive ways of the past. For example, sophisticated international telephone systems, computers, and fax machines greatly simplified the process of writing this book. My heart does not long to go back to simple pen and paper! Yet each of these technical advances can also be used in ways that complicate lives. The problem in this case lies with the person, not the possessions.

Simplicity and simplistic answers are not the same. Oversimplification, like any good taken to excess, is foolishness. The simplicity of discovery that Suzanne experienced while cleaning her medicine chest began with an inward focus and a desire to unify her goals and her heart. Thomas Kelly, author of *A Testament of Devotion,* referred to this focus on the inner life as the "Divine Center." Suzanne recognized the essential harmony between the core of life centered in Christ and the outer circles of influence reflecting His order.

Simplicity of Actions

Many of us are overextended. Our lives are out of focus. We live without any emotional, physical, or financial margins of strength to fall back on. Uncollected, we lack singleness of purpose with which to filter our endeavors.

Because of her new understanding of the harmony between her heart (her inner life) and her actions (her outward life), Suzanne felt the need not only to order her heart, but also to clean her bathroom cabinet.

She lifted down five nearly empty bottles of face and body lotions. How like her; she enjoyed variety and tended to indulge herself by having several things going at once, cluttering up her thoughts and filling every available moment of her time. Suzanne stopped to get a notepad. Across the top of the page she wrote a bold heading: TO SIMPLIFY YOUR LIFE, then on the first line she noted, *Finish one thing before you start into something new.* She poured all the lotion into one squeeze bottle and discarded the others.

Then Suzanne threw all the outdated prescriptions away. Why had she kept them "just in case" when she knew it wasn't healthy? She jotted down, *Keep life current. Don't clutter the present with things that should have been taken care of in the past.*

Next on the shelf were several bottles of perfume—she could never decide which one was her favorite. One bottle of cologne had tipped over in the back and leaked onto everything around it, leaving a discolored brown spot on the shelf. Now she realized her inability to make one decision had resulted in unnecessary choices, extra expense, and a mess. Suzanne reached for her pencil. *Indecision leads to confusion and disorganization. Not making a choice is a poor choice.*

As Suzanne continued to clean the cabinet she shook her head at the row of baby shampoo, her husband's shampoo, her own shampoo, and cream rinses too. She made another note, *Streamline. Don't buy two when one will do. Why make things complicated?*

Suzanne continued to make more notes to herself as she finished the project. *Focus on a few things. Throw out all but the best, then organize the rest.* Suzanne vowed to make the number-one priority of her life to "seek first the kingdom of God and His righteousness. . . ." (Matt. 6:33).

Suzanne laughed as she described the experience. "It was the one and only time that cleaning our bathroom was meaningful and exhilarating!"

I'm not suggesting that everyone who wishes to simplify life should start by cleaning the bathroom, but in our complex society there is an almost universal need for simplicity.

As Suzanne cleaned the medicine cabinet, she stumbled onto a very useful exercise in this process of looking outside for clues to the inward life. The contents of that bathroom cabinet became a metaphor for her life. The particular steps you feel God is urging you to take may not be the same as Suzanne's, but the technique can still be applied. Try it for yourself:

First, think of a word picture for your life. Suzanne saw her life as being like a cluttered bathroom cabinet. Another client, Dewain, remarked, "I'm living my life shotgun-style when I want to be a rifle." Now think of your own analogy.

My life is like a roller coaster when I really desire to be like a boat on a quiet sea. I realize it is not easy to find simplicity. As a friend said, "David, even if your life wasn't a roller coaster and was a boat on a quiet sea, you'd create so much ruckus on that quiet sea that the boat would be just like it was on a roller coaster!" There was great insight in the remark because outer calm must come from inner calm.

_____

_____

_____

Now that you have a clear mental image, consider what made you choose the analogy you did. Why is your life like this metaphor? Suzanne wrote, *because I seem too over-whelmed with all my responsibilities I don't stop and take time to evaluate what I'm doing.*

Why do you think your life seems to be so cluttered?

_____

_____

_____

Now reflect on specific steps you can take to move toward the simpler, more direct life you desire. In the same way Suzanne did, note any insights or directives that stand out to you. I sometimes use as a checklist the ten control-ling principles for the outward expression of simplicity that Richard J. Foster suggests in his classic book *Celebration of Discipline.*[7] I will mention a few of these principles below (and you can check those you might like to adopt). If you decide to actively pursue this fifth step in discovery, you might wish to read Foster's entire book. Please note that these are not legalistic rules, but a guide for those who seek to be liberated by greater simplicity in their lives.

☐ Buy things for their usefulness rather than their status. Cars should be bought for their utility, not their pres-tige.

☐ Reject anything that is producing an addiction in you. Learn to distinguish between a real psychological need, such as cheerful surroundings, and an addiction.

☐ Develop a habit of giving things away. If you find that you are becoming attached to some possession, consider giving it to someone who really needs it. . . . De-accumulate. Masses of unneeded things complicate life.

☐ Look with a healthy skepticism at all "buy-now-pay-later" schemes. They are a trap and serve to deepen your bondage. Certainly prudence as well as simplicity would demand that we use extreme caution before incurring debt.

☐ Reject anything that will lead to the oppression of others. Do we enjoy hierarchical relationships in the company or factory that keep others under us? Do we oppress our children or spouse because certain tasks are beneath us? Often our oppression is tinged with racism and sexism.

Add a few others that will further simplify your own life:

1. _____

2. _____

3. _____

4. _____

Now link each of your specific insights to a short-term goal. For example, you might link the need to consolidate your efforts to the specific goal of hiring someone to do a repair project that's been nagging at your mind. Fill in two or three simple goals with a specific time frame for completion:

	Goal	Completion Date
1.		
2.		
3.		
4.		

This meditation can open up possibilities for new ways of living. It's also a lot of fun to talk about around the kitchen table!

Simplicity of Word

So often we ramble on and on, cluttering our conversations with unnecessary words and complicated jargon. Being direct and concise aids communication and leaves more time for listening. In the Sermon on the Mount, Jesus' instruction book on how to live the Christian life, He urged His listeners to keep things simple. "Let your 'Yes' be 'Yes,' and your 'No,' 'No.' For whatever is more than these is from the evil one."[8]

My natural tendency is to speak, even to be verbose. But I have come to realize that my words should be fewer and I should give myself time to listen. Then when I talk, I can speak from the heart, the integrated part of my life, rather than just from my mind.

These principles of simplicity, I've found, can also be applied to our professions and vocations. Sometimes we do not see ourselves or our lives as others see us.

Another exercise that I find very helpful in my work with clients in therapy is a discovery photograph, in which the clients get a kind of feedback from people who have been intimately involved in their discovery work. For example, the clients may get feedback from the therapist, spiritual director, pastor, or friend they meet with. The clients ask those friends to paint a picture of how they see the clients. Then the clients consider whether they agree with how the people see them.

Simplicity of Vocation

There is a vast need for simplicity in the workplace and at the institutional, governmental, and social-service levels. This is especially evident in the ethical dilemmas related to human services that involve increasing demand and limited resources. As I mentioned earlier, in 1984 I was given the responsibility of developing a comprehensive approach to the severe crack-cocaine epidemic facing the Bahamas. I remember feeling overwhelmed by the burgeoning needs of the hurting men and women in our midst. At that time psychiatric textbooks stated that cocaine was a relatively harmless drug with low addictive power, and few people believed we had a problem. The major question was how to chart the epidemic scientifically to create a groundswell of public and private support for developing educational and treatment programs.

Consultation with some of the leading drug epidemiological researchers in the United States led to a resounding conclusion that any decent study would be extremely expensive and would still have questionable validity. Perplexed and concerned, I called a colleague at Yale, Professor James Jekel, the Winslow Professor of Public Health and Epidemiology. Professor Jekel flew down to the Bahamas to examine the situation.

After a few days of investigating how to conduct a scientific study, we were still puzzled. That evening around the dining-room table, we prayed about the situation, asking for wisdom to understand the problem. As simple as it is, Professor Jekel came up with the idea of focusing on a study that would look at the number of addicts in treatment. In the study we would interview a number of patients in depth.

By talking with one of the longstanding addicts, Professor Jekel was able to pinpoint the origin of cocaine use, and most importantly, to determine when a dangerous form of cocaine, freebase or crack-cocaine, was first used. Although cocaine entered the Bahamas in 1975, people didn't start coming to the hospital with the pathological symptoms associated with cocaine addiction until 1982. The key factor was the change from cocaine powder to cocaine rock or freebase as the only available form of the drug.

Our study, done in the simplest way with minimal funds, was published as the featured scientific article in the *Lancet* medical journal in 1986, thus documenting the first known epidemic of crack-cocaine. The study, which enabled us to chart the Bahamian cocaine problem, has become a model for the study of crack abuse in any contained community. It was a true example of how the simplicity of heart and action and words—praying, talking to people, and listening intently to them—could answer an ethical dilemma. In contrast, it might be shocking to find out the money and time we lose in human services because of our penchant for the complex rather than the simple.

During the same time period, the National Drug Task Force, which I headed, visited Black Village, an area ravaged by crack-cocaine use. The sight was pathetic. At 11:00 A.M. scores of young men were hanging around an old, broken-down building, smoking cocaine. They refused any offer of rehabilitation. In fact, they made fun of the task-force members. We left the area feeling hopeless, discouraged, and frustrated.

A friend and I began to meet to pray about the problem on Wednesdays at lunchtime. A few weeks later a young man, Ezekiel Munnings, rang my doorbell during that prayer time.

"I have just returned from seminary," Zeke said, "and I am interested in a ministry to young men and women on the streets."

Immediately we shared our concern about the pathos in Black Village. The people there were totally "based out," malnourished, and quasi-paranoid. They would not come into any treatment center. Many were criminals.

Our decision was to go to them, to provide a little food each morning. At first all of us thought that approach was almost too simple, although we knew they needed the food. Since crack-cocaine satiates the appetite center, crack addicts ignore food while bingeing on the drug, and as a result they may go days without eating. Upon crashing, however, they are extremely hungry.

Zeke agreed to start work there the following day. Supported by a group of businessmen, he organized a food-basket program. After a short Scripture reading followed by singing and a prayer, he would serve breakfast sandwiches that were donated by the local restaurant. Thus, every morning a large group of addicts would congregate for the devotional talk and the food. In the space of a month several of the young men were encouraged to come into treatment.

One morning when I went to check on Zeke's work a group of addicts stopped me on the street and accused me of injecting the breakfast sandwiches with some type of drug. Puzzled, I asked what they meant. "Well, Doc, if we hit crack-cocaine after the devotional time and the breakfast, we do not get high."

I have no logical explanation for the effect of those sandwiches. It makes no sense scientifically or psychologically. I can only guess that the addicts were experiencing some kind of transference. A lot of them were young men whose fathers were not there, but their mothers were extremely religious women who had sent them to Sunday school. The singing and praying probably brought back memories of their childhood—and the presence of God's spirit. Those memories counteracted their desire to use drugs, and that conflict may have blocked the high. You can be sure there was no methadone or other drug in those egg sandwiches.

Maintaining Simplicity

The simple life, once established, must be carefully kept. When I lived on the sea and watched the shimmering colors of the water and sunsets, I got a sense that no matter how busy or rushed I was, I had no power over the sea or sky. Regardless of my activity the sun would rise and set, the tide would come in and go out. Maybe that's one reason why watching the water is so relaxing. I observed a simple rhythm in nature and sought to bring my life into line with that.

In the city, I fought a tendency to fall out of touch with the simple basics of life that are always present in a small island community—birth, suffering, love, death. For example, when I lived in the States, I went to one funeral in ten years. When I returned to the island, where I knew and was known by almost everyone, there was a funeral about every two weeks that touched my heart. Death and life were overt, not events swept to the side because of the heavy traffic of life. Here I knew the families. I cried with them over death. I rejoiced with them over birth.

This had a calming effect on me that helped to simplify my motives. When I watched the baptisms, weddings, and funerals I was confronted with the simple basics: *What's the ultimate use of all the hustle and bustle?* In my heart I pondered, *What's really important and worth living for?*

That helped me to set basic goals, which simplified my life.

In the cities where you do not see the cycles of nature so clearly, it is easy to slide into complexities of fake importance. You break away from the simple patterns of life and the intensity of relationships, making it more of an effort to maintain simplicity. But even in the inner city the heart can find true and simple fellowship.

One time, after our program in the Black Village had been going for about six months, I attended one of the services on Wednesday morning to review the situation and have fellowship with some of the addicts. They met inside a wooden shack furnished only with some rusty metal chairs and a wooden bench. There was no altar. One of the men later asked me to feel a bump in his arm—a bullet was still lodged there. Two people had AIDS. There were five of my friends from outside Black Village and about five addicts.

Peter Moore, an Episcopal minister, conducted the service. "We all need God's love," he told the men, "David and Zeke and I, as well as you. We are all sinners, and Christ died for us all." He told the men they could change their lives; they could go for help. "You are still someone. God loves you."

Then he broke the bread—Christ's body broken for us. He gave us the wine—Christ's blood given for us. We all saw the power of Christ's healing, even though our lifestyles were so different. We moved closer to the Holy Other and closer to each other.

There were no elaborate trappings. There was no overt beauty. The ugliness and the tragedy of life were everywhere. But as we broke the bread and shared the cup in memory of the love of Christ, there was a sense of peace and hope. Such simple emblems, but what powerful meaning: These hurt, destroyed human beings personified the image of the suffering of God. We all were strangely moved by the unseen but poignant presence of the One who had redeemed us by His sacrificial death.

Simplicity in society rests on a sound belief in the power of the individual. The ramifications of the life of Jesus Christ touch one heart after another and the world is changed. On the island that day, the simplicity of the Last Supper reached down to a small group of broken people trying to make sense of life. And the story does not stop there.

After years of trying to get my drug-rehabilitation program into the prison, the day finally arrived when my team was allowed to begin. However, due to a holiday weekend, I was the only person who showed up. As the hardened prisoners gathered, I must admit I felt apprehensive and nervous about whether my program would be effective with this group.

Then a tall, well-dressed prison overseer approached me and said, "Don't worry, Doc. We can work it out." I looked up and saw to my amazement that it was Neil, one of the hopeless crack addicts I had met ten years before in Black Village. He had been living in an old car then. Through Zeke and the breakfasts, Neil entered treatment at a Teen Challenge program, and the direction of his life changed forever. Now he was an overseer, a man well known and respected by the prisoners.

For me this was a holy moment when the good, the true, and the beautiful manifested themselves. Who could have told me ten years ago that Neil, one of the hopeless addicts we had come to serve, would open the way for a ministry to crack addicts in the prison? Yet Neil was there as an indispensable part of God's plan and a minister of encouragement to me. All this is simple, but at the same time most profound.

Or should I say miraculous?

11

A Spirit of Blessing:
Willingness to Serve and
to Be Served

A few years ago, as I was walking through the public ward of the hospital in Nassau I passed a disheveled older woman whose face was deeply weathered by the wind and rain of life. Feeling led to speak to her, I asked how she was feeling. With soft speech, thick with a European accent, she blurted out her story: Her husband had been killed in World War II, her two sons had been killed in a car accident, and she had terminal cancer. While at home in Holland she had seen pictures of the beautiful beaches in the Bahamas and decided she would travel to Nassau to spend her last few months of life here.

I was dumbfounded—shocked and overwhelmed with the pathos and pain of her story. The Dutch lady, who introduced herself as simply Johanna, continued to talk. She was extremely lonely, sad, and angry at the cards life had dealt her. As we looked at each other the nonverbal communication was *Why?* Why had this happened to her? It was painful to listen to her life story, let alone to be trapped, as she was, in such a tragic script. I wanted to extend an offer of friendship to Johanna before I moved on in my rounds so I invited her to drop by some Sunday evening, when we have a small open house, for a cup of tea at our seaside home.

Continuing my busy schedule in the days that followed, I forgot about the invitation. A few Sundays later, at about 7 P.M., the doorbell rang. My wife answered the door and a woman with a Dutch-English accent said Dr. Allen had invited her to drop by for tea. By now I, too, was at the door greeting her. We invited her to sit with us by the sea. As the waves pounded the shore, ringing out their music of power and majesty, Johanna repeated her tragic story of loneliness and despair; her hazel eyes, flecked with gray, reflected deep suffering.

Although the story was still painful for me, I felt a sense of peace and hope as we looked out at the beauty of the sea. After a time of talking quietly, I read the Sunday-evening Scripture, a tradition in our home. I then told Johanna the story of Jesus coming into the world to express God's love to us personally.

After listening for a while, Johanna said quietly with a pained expression, "That sounds beautiful. But I can't believe it. It is only a fairy tale."

Our hearts went out to her. She became a regular guest in our home on Sunday evenings. We felt God was calling us to serve her in some special way.

Willingness to Serve and to Receive

A willingness to serve and to receive is the sixth attitude of the heart. Unfortunately we tend to pass service by more times than we would care to admit. We haven't the time or energy for problems other than our own. It is easy to allow ourselves to become too businesslike, too professional, too efficient—until we become inflexible. We are unwilling to set aside our own agendas to help others when the need arises. We walk around the problems in our paths in order to accomplish our own goals.

Our reasoning often provides us a quick and easy way to rationalize our actions. Some of the more common forms of this flawed reasoning include ethical narcissism, ethical hedonism, ethical relativism, ethical authoritarianism, and utilitarianism.

Consider how each message, communicated through culture and media, has influenced your own code of behavior.

Ethical Narcissism

According to Lawrence Kohlberg, one of my mentors at Harvard, the earliest and most infantile form of moral reasoning is ethical narcissism, or, in the vernacular, "All for me, baby. I'm going to take care of me. Numero uno. It's a matter of survival of the fittest."[1]

In this immature stage of moral development, we have no interest in serving others—unless, of course, it brings benefit to us. In the story of the Good Samaritan, the men who walked by the wounded man are examples of this ethical narcissism.

Ethical Hedonism

The second level of moral development is ethical hedonism: "Life is a mess, but get what you can get out of it. Eat, drink, and be merry for tomorrow we die." This "grab-the-gusto" ethic leaves little room for service because we are too busy gratifying our own desires to meet the needs of others.

Ethical Relativism

Third is ethical relativism: "Take care of your own. Help those who are part of your family, your group, your race—folks like you—and just forget the rest." This mind-set allows for limited service to those who qualify, but leads to selfish exploitation or oppression of one group by another, which overrules brotherly compassion.

Ethical Authoritarianism

Fourth is ethical authoritarianism, otherwise known as "the Watergate stage." This flawed reasoning says, "Yes, sir, I know it was wrong, but the president ordered it." "Yes, I know my vocation says I should take care of my kids, but the job demands my time." At this level we may recognize our responsibility to serve our fellow man but we rationalize our way out of it. Excuses, excuses, excuses.

Utilitarianism

The fifth level is utilitarianism, the greatest good for the greatest number of people—or for the most powerful people. This is fantastic if you are part of the "in" group, but no one is really safe because standards may shift, making you no longer one of the privileged. Service for the least among us is not part of this plan.

The truth is that none of these flawed ethics works. We all know that. My conviction is that in our culture we need an ethic that brings about the meaning of community and personal values of service to our families, neighbors, and world. This ethic is reflected in Christ's direction to us at the Last Supper and His well-known parable of the Good Samaritan.

Serve One Another

After washing the disciples' feet, Christ explained the meaning of this loving gesture. "If I then, your Lord and Teacher, have washed your feet, you also ought to wash one another's feet. For I have given you an example, that you should do as I have done to you."[2] What a powerful model. But obviously this is not the popular way. It was never meant to be the pathway of the majority. Instead, Christ was presenting a unique form of leadership.

Jesus knew from experience that the way of the earth is hard, fraught with struggle, tears, and tragedy. And those who would grasp the meaning of life must be willing to listen to the pain, soothe the hurt, and wash the feet of fellow travelers. Jesus had shown the disciples what He meant by serving one another in the parable of the Good Samaritan.

The Good Samaritan Ethic of Service

The Good Samaritan ethic is simple and basic. Think about these five components of the parable Jesus told.[3]

1. The Good Samaritan had the ability to get down off his donkey.

We need to get off our donkeys of arrogance, political difference, self-righteousness, or whatever else keeps us from getting our hands dirty by helping others. That's what the Czepaneks did.

One Sunday evening, several weeks after Johanna had first started coming to our home, I noticed she was weaker and did not look well. I realized the cancer was slowly claiming her strength, although in true European fashion she was putting up a good fight. That same evening a newly married, middle-aged couple, the Czepaneks, visited us for the first time. Mr. Czepanek, a banker, shared how he and his wife wanted their lives to express the meaning of God's love, as Christ's did. His statements were marked by sincerity and deep conviction, and no bragging rights.

Johanna listened quietly to his carefully chosen words and his wife's gentle conversation. Later in the evening, when she shared her story I noticed Mr. Czepanek looking at his wife, but I had no idea what their nonverbal communication meant.

After the time of prayer, he moved beside Johanna. "We have a spare room in our house," he said, "and my wife and I would like you to live with us."

It was a holy moment. I was deeply moved by this couple's willingness to reach out to a dying woman. After much persuasion, Johanna agreed to live with them.

2. The Good Samaritan ethic builds community.

Secondly the Good Samaritan ethic builds community. It's an ethic of universal love—love that allows the Samaritan, the different one, to move to the wounded man. Who is my neighbor that I am to love as myself? Every man, woman, and child merits this brotherly love. John, the heroin addict in Boston. Monica, the blonde model whose baby had died. Johanna, the old Dutch woman who was dying of cancer.

The Good Samaritan ethic means accepting those who are different from us—even if they may not have accepted us. Samaritans were hated and despised by many in their culture, yet this man did not return injustice in kind. Instead, he rose above the moral climate around him and reached out to serve.

While traveling in Africa, I met a missionary doctor of unusually deep knowledge. He told me that when he had first arrived at the hospital, he had plunged into the work and was soon overwhelmed by all the needs. Within a few months he was feeling burned out and feared his own health might break. One Friday a Hindu colleague told him to leave the hospital and take his family to a nearby resort for the weekend. Arriving at the resort, the doctor found all expenses had been paid by the Hindu doctor. In his room was a fully stocked refrigerator. As a result of that restorative weekend, the missionary received fresh vigor and hope to press on.

Even years later, the missionary doctor was moved to tears as he told me about the thoughtful act of kindness on the part of his Hindu colleague, a man whose beliefs and background were so different from his own.

3. The Good Samaritan ethic is an ethic of compassion.
The Samaritan saw the wounded man and had compassion on him. The unveiled heart identifies with others and empathizes with their pain. This motivates service.

The apostle Paul warned that although we give the ultimate service ("giving our bodies to be burned") if we do not serve from the heart ("have not love"), it is useless.[4] How paradoxical! Surely if someone sacrifices his or her body, it must be considered good. Not so! God, the final Evaluator of the seen and hidden, judges the motivation of the heart.

How important it is, then, that our motivation for service flows from our heart. This means that our hearts must be liberated—unbound and unblocked. It means seeking forgiveness and giving up our prejudices, hurts, and resentments. It means moving toward service that springs from being a child of God.

Sometimes it is implied that prayer and service are contradictory. This is the Mary-Martha dualism all over again. Either we have to be sitting at Jesus' feet, listening to His wisdom, as Mary was, or preparing dinner for our guests, as Martha was.

How naive, how infantile. Prayer is our source of wisdom

and strength, which equips us to serve. True prayer, like the heartfelt prayers of the Czepaneks for Johanna, is inseparable from the actions that flow from the heart.

Effective service is prayerful service, praying in the heart before and while we serve. Too often we rush about doing things that were never God's idea in the first place. In prayer we discern how to serve others according to God's will, in His time, and in His way.

Thus prayerful service is compassionate service, which means putting ourselves in the place of others and treating them as we ourselves would want to be treated. For me as a psychiatrist it means treating patients as I would want myself or my family to be treated.

Such service moves beyond mere craft to become an art, redemptive and inspiring. All professions, in fact all activities, have a body of knowledge and a "right" way of being performed. Compassionate service must learn the craft— the *modus operandi*—of the profession. But it must not stop there. The challenge is to perform the activity so that it draws the person into community with the servant.

I will never forget a very godly man, a church elder, astute businessman, and natural leader, whom I had always respected in my local fellowship. For many years he and his wife had encouraged individuals and couples in their spiritual journey, and at age eighty he was as active as ever. Then one morning his wife woke up dazed and confused. She repeatedly asked him, "Where am I? Who are you?" It turned out she was in the beginning stages of Alzheimer's disease.

As she became progressively worse and could no longer be cared for at home, he sold their home and moved into a nursing home with her. There he fed her, read to her, and took her for walks each day. What a picture of commitment and service.

One day we had lunch together and he shared with me

how hard his wife's illness had been to endure. In his career he had always been a tough businessman with little tolerance or understanding for weakness or failure. He saw this opportunity to serve his wife in her illness as a way to learn compassion, and he felt this was a lesson God wanted him to learn before he died.

4. The Good Samaritan ethic gives us the courage to confront the problem with appropriate service.

When people realize they have a divine mission to perform—to help someone else—they can move to meet the need in spite of the danger of ridicule, misunderstanding, rejection, and potential physical harm. The Levite and the priest walked on by because they were balcony people who were put off by ridicule and rejection. But not the Samaritan! Since his people were looked down upon by the Jews he was used to standing up for what he believed despite ridicule. He did not care what others thought.

The Samaritan was also prepared to help. He took out his oil and bandages and cared for the wounded man. Then he took the injured man to the inn to provide continued care. The Samaritan follows through, yet involves others as needed.

The Czepaneks served Johanna in this way. They decorated a room for her and made it very comfortable. In the next weeks Johanna became very weak and never returned to my home. A community nurse from the hospital, who also attended our Sunday-evening gatherings, was able to visit her daily. As Johanna's body grew weaker, the Czepaneks fed her, read to her, and took care of her physical needs.

In a very deep sense, to know and worship God in a mature spirituality means committing our lives to service and duty rather than being controlled by the whims of feelings and circumstances. It is often easier to serve ourselves, but at the Last Supper Christ taught that true meaning and ful-

fillment in life, and into eternity, is allowing the love of
God to be expressed through us in service to others. It is a
willing service, rushing forth from hearts overflowing with
love and centered in Christ, not a compulsive or obligatory
set of actions clothed in drudgery. This is the opposite of
codependency, which is not done to please the other person.

As Saint Francis said long ago, "It is in giving that we
receive."

5. The Good Samaritan ethic deals with accountability.

Before the Samaritan left the inn, he said, "Here's some
money, but when I come back I'll pay more if needed. I take
responsibility."

This ethic of serving others rests on our sense of accountability to God, to our own convictions, to our families, and to our fellow human beings.

How About You?

Can you think of a time when you served someone in
need without reimbursement?

Serving one another may be as simple as taking time to
listen. One Sunday morning after my adult Sunday school
class a woman with tears in her eyes came over to my car. I
had been speaking on the hurt trail and the need to keep
our hearts open in worshiping the Holy Other. The lady
told me her husband had suffered a severe head injury and
as a result had lost control of his sphincter muscles. That
morning he had soiled his pants, as he often did. Frustrated
and angry at the unfairness of the injury, she sobbed, "I
can't take it anymore . . . I just can't go on like this."

Seeing the pain in her face, I inwardly cringed because I
felt so helpless. What could I do for her? Even as a medical
doctor and a psychiatrist trained in neurology, I had very
little hope or help to offer her.

As she continued crying and holding my arm I realized again that I did not have to be God. I did not have to fix every problem or solve every situation. The gift I could offer was to listen to her, to cry with her, to pray with her. At that particular moment, she needed someone to care about what she was going through.

Now it's your turn to think about a time when you served someone else:

_____

_____

_____

Write how you felt as you performed this service:

_____

_____

_____

Why did you do this? My answer was this:

Ever since I walked my own path to discovery I have wanted to help others express their pain so they can open their hearts to love and be loved.

Why did _you_ do this for this particular person?

_____

_____

_____

Discovery is enhanced by serving others out of love and compassion. Some opportunities for service in your community may include:

- Your family and employer
- The environment

- Mentally retarded persons
- Drug-rehabilitation organizations
- Physically handicapped persons
- The elderly
- AIDS patients
- Volunteer projects in a hospital, housing district, or community sports teams

We may be called to menial, trivial, mundane acts of service. Our children, our spouses, our neighbors, our friends, and our enemies are hurt and bruised by the cares of life. They need us in a thousand little ways: Common courtesy, careful listening, respect.

As Christ said, "Inasmuch as you did it to one of the least of these My brethren, you did it to Me."[5]

Service to Those Who Are Difficult to Care For

We are touched by the humility, grace, and love of our Lord as He washed the feet of His disciples, but most amazing must have been His interaction with Judas. As He washed Judas's feet, I can see Him pause and look up, straight into his eyes, as if to say, *Judas, I love you. Are you sure you want to do what you plan to do?*

As caring persons it may seem reasonable to wash the feet of someone who needs us, loves us, and appreciates us. But it may seem superhuman to wash the feet of someone who has kicked us in the teeth.

How many of us reject those who don't like us or won't go along with our program? Not so with Christ. He washed the feet of *all* of His disciples, even those who would deny and betray Him. Is this not the test of love? We are called to serve even those who seem unlovable or who have rejected us.

A quiet chap named Dan did just that. Dan's friend, Robert, a likable, intense young man with deep-set eyes and a square chin, became emotionally ill. As he became more of a hermit and difficult to get along with, most of Robert's friends backed away—all except for Dan. Instead of talking about how difficult Robert had become, Dan prayed for Robert day in and day out. Yet he couldn't convince Robert to get the help he needed.

Still, Dan did not give up. He visited Robert every Sunday, showing love by giving him money, straightening up his home, and encouraging him. Sometimes Robert would get so angry he ran Dan out of his house. Yet for two years straight Dan came every Sunday.

Dan was finally able to win Robert's confidence and convince him to seek professional help. When I commended Dan for his loving persistence, he just shrugged. "Robert wasn't himself. Anyone could see that," he said. "I knew there had to be a chemical imbalance behind the changes. He needed a doctor."

The call to serve is no mean responsibility. Active love has far reaching consequences. And in order to truly serve, we must also be willing to receive.

To Belong You Must Be Willing to Receive

Kneeling with the towel and basin of water, Christ proceeded to wash His disciples' feet. Peter represented each of us when he asked a question of incredulity, "Lord, are You washing my feet?" The answer was obvious; Jesus had already washed other disciples' feet. Then Peter protested, "You shall never wash my feet." Obviously Peter was disturbed by the role of his leader. In his mind he just could not see a man of authority taking the role of a servant. Could he follow a leader who was willing to stoop so low?

Then Christ answered, "If I do not wash you, you have no part with Me."[6]

In essence, Christ was saying to Peter, "If you want to belong, you have to be willing to receive what I have to give." A lot of us, particularly men, can give, but we find it very hard to receive. And we find it even more difficult to say, "Thank you," or "I appreciate you." Christ is saying that when you discover your potential in life, you will realize it is not only in giving, but also in having the ability to receive.

Imagine what would happen today if you turned to your boss, your wife, or even your children and said, "I really appreciate you. Thank you for your help."

If you think this would surprise them, ask yourself some questions about your openness toward others:

☐ Can you receive their love?
☐ Their advice?
☐ Their forgiveness?

Now imagine the situation in reverse, where someone you know well expresses his or her appreciation of you. Can you receive a compliment?

One-sided independence damages our sense of community, just as one-sided codependency does. As I mentioned earlier, we are created to be interdependent, each one giving and receiving from others. The meeting of one another's needs knits us together.

Rick, a reserved gentlemen who prided himself on his reputation for being a hard worker, lost his job due to economic recession and soon ran through his savings. He felt scared. But most of all, he did not feel like a man. He hated himself. The lowest point in his life was when his wife asked him to bring home some milk for the baby—and he did not have the courage to tell her he was totally out of money.

Terrified with worry, Rick walked around town, hoping

he could somehow work out the situation. He circled a grocery store owned by his friend, but could not bring himself to ask his friend for help. He felt like a failure. When he returned home without the milk, his wife simply walked next door and borrowed some from the neighbor. No big deal.

Even as Rick told this story several years later, he trembled with fear. "I never want that to happen again. I hate being that vulnerable, that out of control."

I gently pointed out that his wife had a healthier outlook. Her worth as a person was not threatened by the give-and-take of neighborly helpfulness; no thought was given to being more or less valuable as a person because of exchanging favors. Giving as well as receiving bonded her to her friends.

Although matters of the heart are never simple, I would suggest that two common issues are often at the core of an unwillingness to receive. First, you may feel unworthy to receive because you don't understand that your identity and dignity are gifts of grace—neither earned nor deserved on the basis of perceived merit.

Second, you may resist receiving because of the unwillingness to be bonded or identified with the other person. Pride, fear, dislike, or distrust may make you resistant to any service or love the other person may offer—regardless of how sincere and constructive the service may be. Prayerful discernment is needed to discover the healthy balance of serving and receiving.

A grateful heart qualifies you to become a healer . . . a repairer of the breach . . . a builder of broken walls. Only when you are vulnerable to receive can you truly give. Church leaders, pastors, and lay people often want to be seen as examples of the victorious life, as people who "have it all together." Instead, could it be that the Lord is calling us to be "wounded healers," admitting our pain and being willing to receive help when it is offered? Are we willing to admit our needs or to receive correction even from those who are in our care?

Jesus was teaching the basic lesson of His kingdom, that the greatest or the most powerful must be the servant of all. Our Lord told Peter in no uncertain terms that if He could not wash Peter's feet, Peter could not be His partner. Shocked, Peter replied that if that were the case, he wanted Jesus to wash his whole body.

Christ lovingly told him, "He who is bathed needs only to wash his feet, but is completely clean; and you are clean. . . ."[7] Again Christ told him that since he was already committed and cleansed, only his feet required washing, which signified Christ's service to him.

Peter needed the continuing forgiveness, support, and care of Christ to continue his pilgrimage. How many of the faithful today feel they can go it alone, depending on a previous commitment or ecstatic experience from the past? How erroneous! Unless we have the continual refreshing and cleansing touch of God these spiritual experiences will fade.

True spirituality requires the daily experience of having our feet washed through:

- Prayer ("Come to Me, all you who labor and are heavy laden, and I will give you rest."[8])
- Reading the Scriptures ("the washing of water by the word" [9])
- Confession and cleansing ("If we confess our sins, He is faithful and just to forgive us our sins and to cleanse us from all unrighteousness."[10])
- Caring, reciprocal, servant fellowship ("Bear one another's burdens, and so fulfill the law of Christ."[11])

Christ set the example Himself.

Christ Was Willing to Receive

Shortly before the crucifixion, while Jesus was at the house of Simon, the leper, a woman came in and anointed Him with a costly jar of perfume. The disciples were shocked and expected Jesus to restrain her. "To what purpose is this waste?" they asked. "For this fragrant oil might have been sold for much and given to the poor."

Instead Jesus received what she had done with gratitude. "Why do you trouble the woman? For she has done a good work for Me.... For in pouring this fragrant oil on My body, she did it for My burial. Assuredly, I say to you, wherever this gospel is preached in the whole world, what this woman has done will also be told as a memorial to her."[11]

Jesus knew what had been done, He knew the sacrifice, and He appreciated it. He gratefully received this woman's precious love and caring actions.

In the letter to the Philippians, the apostle Paul expressed his deep gratitude to the believers who had sacrificially supported him with monetary gifts and by sending Epaphroditus to minister to him. It must have been a real encouragement to them to know they had been a blessing to their spiritual father. Today, by contrast, even the simple courtesy of expressing appreciation or sending thank-you notes is often forgotten.

During our Lord's mission on earth He healed many people. In one incident, He healed ten lepers. But only one leper returned to thank Him. Christ asked, "Where are the other nine?" His question was a powerful statement that implied the other nine were missing something. Their healing was incomplete. Gratitude is a reflection of an open, overflowing heart. The cure of the leprosy was a powerful miracle, but the opening of a closed heart to faith and gratitude is the quintessential meaning of life. People like to feel needed. Be willing to accept what others

have to offer. And let them know you appreciate that help.
Christ calls us to serve others. He calls us to receive service from others. And we are blessed, ourselves, when we
do so.

The Fulfillment of Service

After Jesus had girded Himself with the towel and
washed the feet of His disciples, He explained His actions.
"If I then, your Lord and the Teacher, have washed your
feet, you also ought to wash one another's feet. For I have
given you an example, that you should do as I have done to
you. . . . If you know these things, happy are you if you do
them"[12]

One translation uses the word *blessed* instead of *happy*
in this passage. *Blessed* is a word little used in our modern
vocabulary. It means a sense of inner peace, fulfillment,
happiness, and joy. It is not a transitory state, dependent on
a chemical high or a happy lot in life. It is a sense of knowing that all is well in life and death, in joy and sorrow, in
sickness and in health.

This fulfillment is perhaps most relevant to those like
Johanna who are intimately acquainted with suffering. It
implies a particular relationship with God: finding our
resting and abiding place in Him. It is the experience of the
psalmist who could say, "The LORD is my light and my
salvation; / Whom shall I fear?"[13]

In his book *Making Sense Out of Suffering*, Peter Kreeft
helps us understand the meaning of happiness or blessedness:

The meaning of the word happiness has changed since
Aristotle's time. We usually mean by it today something
wholly subjective, a feeling. If you feel happy, you are
happy. But Aristotle and nearly all pre-modern writers

meant that happiness was an objective state first of all, not merely a subjective feeling. The Greek word for happiness, Eudaimia, literally means good spirit or good soul. To be happy is to be good. Therefore, by this definition Job in his suffering is happy. Socrates condemned to die is happy. Hitler exulting over the conquest of France is not happy. Happiness is not a warm puppy. Happiness is goodness.[14]

Addressing a group of children, Albert Schweitzer said, "I don't know what your destiny will be but one thing I know, the only ones among you who will be really happy are those who have sought and found a way to serve."[15]

Our family felt happiness and fulfillment during an especially memorable Christmas holiday. Before the Czepaneks met Johanna, my wife and I wanted to serve her by offering companionship to ward off the loneliness of her life. We invited her to come to our home for Christmas and share the festivities with our family. She arrived at our home wearing a becoming dress, her pale complexion brightened with soft makeup. Although her appearance gave an illusion of health and cheer, Johanna seemed to instinctively know it would be her last Christmas and she had dressed to show how special it was. The evening was sacred as we all shared a beautiful dinner and Johanna told us stories of her family.

The Czepaneks also experienced the tremendous satisfaction and fulfillment that results from service. Obviously, they could not reach out to each and every hurting person on the island. But they were sensitive to the leading of the Holy Spirit and met Johanna's needs in a tender, loving way. The fulfillment they felt in return was much more than the passing pleasures money can buy or the happiness achieved through selfish pursuits.

I suggest that each of us can discover fulfillment as we devote ourselves to the vocation to which God has called us, as the Czepaneks did. Not all of us will care for the terminally ill or counsel drug addicts or teach children. But each one of us will be called to significant labor for the kingdom. As we discover our true potential and do the things we are particularly suited to do, service becomes a repository of happiness and joy.

Fulfillment is not an all-or-nothing accomplishment. We cannot take steps one, two, three, and wake up in the morning with lasting fulfillment. Again we are talking about a journey of spiritual discovery toward increased personal growth and satisfying labor. Longfellow in his poem, "A Psalm of Life," wrote:

> Not enjoyment, and not sorrow,
> Is our destined end or way;
> But to act, that each to-morrow
> Finds us farther than to-day.[16]

The very real condition of fulfilled living in Christ does not mean, however, that the road to true happiness and blessedness is without hassles, frustrations, rejection, or failure. People will disagree, criticize, misinterpret our motives, and even openly reject us.

Jesus warned us about such times in the Sermon on the Mount when He said:

> Blessed are those who are persecuted for righteousness' sake, for theirs is the kingdom of heaven. Blessed are you when they revile and persecute you, and say all kinds of evil against you falsely, for My sake. Rejoice and be exceedingly glad, for great is your reward in heaven, for so they persecuted the prophets who were before you.[17]

At such times we receive solace through the vision of God and His kingdom, for He will never leave nor forsake us.

This experience of finding fulfillment in the midst of rejection or pain is the gift of God. It is this joy that the angels sang to the shepherds when the baby Jesus was born. And coming full circle at the end of His life, it was because of the anticipated joy of our eternal salvation that Christ endured the cross. Joy and fulfillment are not experienced _apart_ from pain but _beyond_ it. Like Jesus, we will find that the completion of our inner fulfillment comes independently of the visible results or the response of others to our work.

Johanna's life was a powerful sermon for me. Her sincere quest for the love of God was not met by the church or even by my Scripture reading, although that may have helped. The expression of God's love came to her in the couple who figuratively and literally washed her feet. The Czepaneks' love become tangible joy for her in the midst of her suffering and meaning in the midst of tragedy. Johanna received the reality of the loving service Christ called us to when He said, "For I was hungry and you gave Me food; I was thirsty and you gave Me drink; I was a stranger and you took Me in."[18]

A few weeks after Johanna became confined to her bed at the Czepanek home, I was walking down Bay Street and heard someone call me. It was Mr. Czepanek. "Johanna died last week," he told me. Then he described how things had gone since they had taken her in and how joyful she had become at the end. His eyes misted over as he related their parting conversation. As Johanna was dying she said, "Tell David Jesus is real. It is not a fairy tale."

❧12❧

A Spirit of Eternity: A Transcendent Perspective

In the spring of 1977, while I was teaching at Yale Divinity School, I received news that my mother was not feeling well and would need an operation. I immediately flew to Nassau to be with her, arriving just before she went into surgery. My mother had always been a strong, vibrant figure in my life, so it was terribly difficult to see her weak and ill. She lifted her arm up from the starched white sheets and took my hand. After a moment she began in a quiet, calm voice to recite Psalm 23: "The LORD is my Shepherd; / I shall not want. . . ."

When she came to the part, "Yea though I walk through the valley of the shadow of death, / I will fear no evil; / For Thou art with me," Mother pressed my hand tightly in hers. Then she was wheeled away from me into surgery.

After the operation my mother returned to her hospital room and I was allowed to visit her. She kept straining to talk to me, but I encouraged her to rest and reassured her that we could talk in the morning. Mother relaxed against her pillow, but she kept wanting to talk.

My medical training kicked in, and I encouraged her to lie back, let the doctors do their work, and allow her body time to rest. Later in the evening as I was leaving, Mother still wanted to speak. But again I told her to get a good night's sleep and I would be back early in the morning. We could talk then.

I was restless all night and could not sleep well. About 5:30 that morning I received a call from the hospital, informing me that Mother had died. I wanted to somehow turn back the clock. Upon reflection, I thought she might have wanted to talk of death—but I hadn't wanted to hear that. She needed rest, my medical mind informed me. As a boy I knew how to listen to my mother; as a man I thought I knew more important things.

"Where is the life we have lost in living? Where is the wisdom we have lost in knowledge?" wrote T. S. Eliot.[1]

A Life Beyond This One

So often in our lives, we become automatons; our lives lose meaning. In contrast, *transcendence* means that in the midst of ordinary life, God's love is present. So there's more to me than David Allen. My life becomes a vehicle to express the love of God in my heart and in the world. Your life has meaning beyond daily living also.

I first realized this at my niece Fern's funeral. As the service for her and Bradley continued, I felt a sense of inspiration. Fern's life had ended; she'd made her statement. Now the challenge was, *What is my life all about? What is the message of my life?*

The other thought that came was that in the spiritual sense our lives assume different characteristics. It's almost as if we develop a spiritual name that is different from our physical name. Fern's name was Fern. But as I thought of her, she could be called Faithfulness, Beauty, or Grace. I could think of others who, as I looked at their lives, could be called Persistence or Encouragement.

It seems to me that the meaning of life is to move through our spiritual development so that we transcend our so-called physical bodies, even our given names, to move into what I call spiritual reality, or the eternal perspective.

As I sat there at the funeral I kept asking myself, *David? What will David represent?* The name David means "beloved," and one of my goals in life is to know more of the meaning of love. In one sense Love and Compassion and Mercy are the spiritual names I hope to have, the messages of who I am and what I see and what I do.

As Longfellow wrote:

> Lives of great men all remind us
> We can make our lives sublime,
> And, departing, leave behind us
> Footprints on the sands of time.[2]

In some ways Fern had completed her mission. The question now was, *How was I to develop spiritually?* Her funeral became a powerful inspiration to me.

As C. S. Lewis said, "There are no mere people." Transcendence means the reality that life is pregnant with God's love in people, in activities, and in nature. Christ told us this at the end of the Last Supper.

Christ's Teaching of Transcendence

After extolling the virtue of true service in following His example of washing His disciples' feet, Christ said, "I say to you, he who receives whomever I send receives Me; and he who receives Me receives Him who sent Me."³ Jesus was telling the disciples they would be seeing *Him* when they saw each other. In a unique way the incarnation of God in human form happened only once—when "the Word became flesh and dwelt among us."⁴ But in another sense the incarnation continues as Christ is embodied in our lives. When we choose to commit our lives to Him and receive His forgiveness, we are recreated and His Spirit comes to live within us. We are made new in Christ; our bodies become the sanctuary of the Holy God.⁵ This is the mystery Paul spoke of when he wrote, "Christ in you, the hope of glory."⁶

His Spirit relates intimately with our spirits, giving evidence in our heart that God is with us. What a thought! Therefore in an even deeper way you are more than you are, and I am more than I am. Life has dimensions beyond what we see and feel in this present moment.

People in discovery see people as who they are, but more than that, as representative of the living Christ. They see a situation as painful, but by stepping back they can see the meaning in it. Beyond the material there is a powerful spiritual reality.

What a difference it would make if, instead of seeing our spouse, our child, our friend . . . even our enemy, we could recognize transcendence—and see the image of Jesus. In this light, there are no hopeless people. Everybody has something to teach us. And no one can separate us from the presence of Christ.

One Friday when I had just completed my rounds at Knowles House Community Clinic in Nassau, the chief nurse informed me we had just been alerted about a tragedy. A poor mother had gone to buy food, leaving her four sleeping children alone in the house. While she was gone, the house burned down and three of the children died in the blaze.

The distraught mother and the lone surviving child, an eight-year-old girl, were brought to see me. Working in a busy emergency clinic, I was accustomed to being involved with many tragedies. However, as this story unfolded, the pathos and misfortune of this poor family gripped my heart. How would this little girl cope with the tragedy? Surely it would destroy her. I, and others, prayed hard on her behalf.

As I counseled the child during the next three months, I was amazed. She had a particular grace about her. Yes, she cried and was sad, but she exuded a sense of hope. She talked openly about missing her dead brothers and sister. She drew pictures of their graves. She dreamed of them, had nightmares of the fire, and often admitted she was frightened. Occasionally she could not sleep and had to be given a small amount of antihistamine to help her. But as I sat with her, she exuded hope and peace.

What a beautiful smile. Looking at her, I felt a sense of awe. Before long I realized she was teaching me, showing me there is transcendence.

Is it presumptuous to suggest that God's love gives grace to the suffering? Could it be that the presence of Christ is the real therapeutic dynamic? How else do the poor survive? How else do children like this little girl—and like Lisa, my niece's daughter—who have experienced such horror, seem so healthy?

Earlier in my career, when I was at Harvard, I was closed to this possibility, as I shared with you in the first chapter of this book. But after traveling throughout the world and feeling the pain of my brethren, it is now easier to believe than not to. I have witnessed God's work among us! In the lives of Joan and Sir Lambert and Dr. Mendez—and hundreds of others who have been my patients and my friends.

Transcendence is not optional; it is essential for survival if life is to have meaning.

How comforting to know that we have a Higher Power who cares about our hurts and pain. We have this exquisite treasure, the very presence of God, in our own hearts, earthly jars of clay, so that our hope and power may be from God and not of ourselves. "If God is for us, who can be against us?"[7]

The good, the true, and the beautiful go together, but this does not mean we're to have a rose-colored view of life. This was pointed out to me by Roland Johnson, a sculptor working in a small art gallery in the isolation of the Abaco islands of the Bahamas. Showing me a sculpture of a haggard old lady (representing death) chasing a virile young man (representing life), he explained that although the sculpture is tragic, it is true and therefore beautiful. "The sculpture forces us to face the reality of life," he said, "and recognize the need for a philosophy that transcends the tragedy of death through eternal life." In a later piece of art, this sculptor captured his own journey toward faith in a beautiful bronze of Mary at the tomb of the risen Christ.

In light of the transcendent glory of God, the earth blossoms with a vibrant beauty and hope. When we believe, we do not have to go far to see or hear the message of God's love and splendor. Blake describes the universal beauty evident in the microcosms of creation:

> To see a world in a grain of sand,
> And Heaven in a wild flower,
> Hold infinity in the palm of your hand,
> And eternity in an hour.[8]

The reminders of transcendence are all around us, but we need to open our hearts each day to see them. I hope that's what we've done in this book. But spiritual discovery is, as I mentioned at the beginning of the book, a process.

Maintaining Spiritual Discovery

Each day we recommit ourselves to be missionaries to our own hearts. And each month or so we need to give our spiritual growth a checkup. The following exercise may help you evaluate your progress.

A Spiritual Balance Sheet

Check the statements below that describe your life now:

- ☐ I have faced my inner hurt, worked through my repressed emotions, and started the process of healing my inner self.
- ☐ I know I have meaning, dignity, identity, and value. I have accepted my authority card from God.
- ☐ I am able to be creative in my relationships, my work, and my play because I allow my real self to emerge.
- ☐ I replace unhealthy familiar patterns of living and problem solving with new and successful ones.
- ☐ I have developed the capacity to experience deeply a wide range of feelings, including positive sentiments.
- ☐ I have developed a strong sense of self-actualization and appropriate assertiveness. I am willing to pursue personal goals and dreams with conviction and determination.
- ☐ I am able to experience closeness with another person with minimal anxiety or fear. I am comfortable expressing myself fully and honestly.
- ☐ I am able to be alone without discomfort because I can nurture myself through memories of past enjoyment.
- ☐ I enjoy solitude, instead of dreading loneliness.
- ☐ I have gotten in touch with my real self, which can now remain stable through varied experiences.

☐ I am able to release the psychic energy that comes from painful experiences through prayer and meditation.

☐ My heart is more grateful, appreciative, and thoughtful. This gives me a more positive attitude.

☐ I am able to be more flexible and adapt to change.

☐ Changes in my lifestyle have occurred that reflect my inner convictions and values.

☐ I have faith in God, which gives me a sense of inner peace and hope.

☐ I experience the presence of God during the day through prayer and Bible reading.

☐ I see God in the faces and concern of my brothers and sisters. I am willing to allow them to serve me.

☐ I express my love of God by serving others and being a steward of the environment.

This short checkup helps me discern if I am moving toward spiritual maturity. Each day I experience discovery through the lives of other people, brothers and sisters like Father John, who was the head of a very distinguished Catholic order in Europe.

While on a sabbatical, Father John spent a year working with me in teaching a course at Yale Divinity School called Psychological Preparation for Ministry, which was designed around a lecture-project-group interaction model. Throughout the year, Father John told us about his struggles in being a priest:

- How hard it was to be celibate in light of extreme temptation
- The increasing demands and the church's decreasing resources
- His struggles with prayer and the seeming absence and silence of God

- His discouragement at seeing the faithful fall by the way and some people revolted by the faith he loved
- His burnout from the myth that the priest is a man for all seasons who can offer total availability, be totally unselfish, and almost superhuman
- His persistent questions about his vocation
- The cruelty and rejection of his brothers in Christ
- His isolation and loneliness in the midst of supposed community
- The gnawing experiences of knowing the good but often doing the opposite

We cried with Father John, we felt his pain, we lived his conflict. In his struggles we saw our own. Was it hopeless? Who would ever dare to enter religious life?

The class members, some of whom were planning to enter the ministry, were amazed, threatened, and downright confused. How could such a distinguished priest, who had served God all these years, still be struggling so intensely—and still be asking if it all was worth it?

Our last class was held as a retreat at the Sisters of Mercy Convent by the sea. At the end we planned a worship and Communion service. For some unknown reason, I felt led to ask Father John to conduct the service.

We were all gathered in the beautiful chapel, the huge glass wall behind the altar revealing the crashing waves of the ocean. With mounting apprehension, I wondered how Father John would handle the service.

At 5:10 P.M. I heard brisk footsteps enter the back of the chapel. I turned to see Father John, dressed in majestic purple robes, triumphantly stride to the altar. After a moment of silence, he addressed the class, "My brothers and sisters, my fellow students, during the past year you saw my pain. You heard my struggles, you saw my tears. You experienced my ambivalence. You empathized with my conflict with celibacy and sexual temptation.

"But I want to tell you today, that in spite of my pain, I have been called to be a priest of the Most High God. A priest I am and a priest I will be by the grace of God."

As Father John led us in worship, everyone was crying. Seeing this brother's pain in the past year had moved us beyond our independent, impenetrable outer selves to face our wounded inner selves. Exposed and wounded, now we were comforted by the body and blood of our Lord, reminding us He took upon Himself our suffering that we would be healed. We no longer saw Father John.

Instead we felt the presence of the transcendent, all-powerful God. And through Father John we had also caught a glimpse of the suffering Christ, made flesh and dwelling among us.

That year, we walked with Father John beyond recovery to spiritual discovery to find a deeper meaning in life, a commitment that goes beyond circumstances, a vocation that surpasses career, and a love of God that transcends our suffering.

After Father John left Yale, he went to live in the jungles of South America, encouraging priests who were called to the poor of that area. Later he was given a worldwide ministry to travel from country to country, strengthening the priests and sisters in remote areas. Like Peter, he was following His Lord, feeding the lambs of God.

Transcendence does not deny the problems of life. It sees the issues head on, counting the cost, feeling the pain. It is amazing grace that goes beyond our limitations to touch the heart of God. My mother's last hours remain a very poignant reminder to me that life is very fragile— transitory. The gift of spending time with each other, the life of the heart, is something we can only share today. We may not have tomorrow.

If you have the chance to be with someone, that is a gift. When we ignore or rush past matters of the heart, for whatever reason, we do so at our peril. Love is not an interruption of what needs to be done. Love is what needs to be done.

My mother taught me to love and to give and to serve from the heart. She is still teaching me. Each day I remember that night is coming, and I tell myself, "Reach out to love Vicki and our children as long as it is day."

My mother and father were ordinary folk who worked day in and day out and often couldn't take a vacation because every penny went for our education. Yet I could see Christ in the midst of their so-called hard life. For them, death meant going on to experience the meaning for which they had lived.

At my mother's funeral my father remained calm and said very little. Then at the grave site he rose, faced the casket, lifted his hand, and said, "Bessie, I salute you. I'll see you in the morning."

I am comforted by the transcendence of eternal life in Christ. My mother and father and I will be reunited. We will talk then.

❧ ❧

Afterword

When I met David Allen in the spring of 1991, my first impression was that he reflected a depth of character well seasoned with humility and sensitivity. I pursued an opportunity to interview him for the position of Chief of Psychiatry at the Minirth-Meier & Byrd Clinic, and eventually my husband and I visited him in his home in Nassau, Bahamas. There, I quickly decided that my initial impression would be a lasting one. Watching him interact with his lovely family and friends confirmed that this was a man who deeply cared about people and their struggles and pursuits for deeper meaning in life—in other words, for *discovery.*

People who meet Dr. Allen discover, as I did, that he is a man with a message, a message *from* the heart *for* the heart. *In Search of the Heart: The Road to Spiritual Discovery* reflects his refreshingly honest approach to exploring the inner life. Throughout the book, Dr. Allen provides the reader with a genuine view of his own search for meaning and authenticity; and in his own disarming manner he encourages readers to take the same journey, to become missionaries to their own hearts, to explore the path of spiritual discovery that leads beyond mediocre existence.

For the last year and a half, Dr. Allen has been presenting the contents of this book to individuals attending Minirth-Meier & Byrd conferences as well as to individuals who are treated in our outpatient counseling and hospital programs. It has been thrilling to see this material encourage powerful growth in so many people, including myself. Consistent feedback seems to show that for many people Dr. Allen's material has been instrumental in pulling life's puzzle pieces together.

At thirty-two years of age, I began to realize my inner life felt empty, despite a loving, evangelical Christian background and the "right" credentials: a lovely Wheaton College undergraduate experience, a Biola University graduate degree, and a fantastic career working to set up the Minirth-Meier & Byrd Clinic in Arlington. Through Dr. Allen's encouragement to explore my own hurt trail and love story, I have been able to connect afresh with the everlasting love of God. I am discovering a new motivation for my vocation and relationships.

It is my hope that this book will have as profound an effect on you as it has had on me and that you will be motivated to take an honest look at your heart—not what *should* be there but what really is there. Perhaps you will uncover your inner anger and begin to see the incredibly destructive and constructive power that lies beneath it. I hope you will embrace anew (or for the very first time) the realization that you are special, made in God's image, and that because God loves you, you have inherent meaning, dignity, identity, and value. These are the threads so poignantly woven throughout this book. My prayer is that you will be encouraged to join others who have begun their journey of discovery and that you will experience the amazing freedom of a life that is open to truth, beauty, and creativity. It is my hope that you will discover your heart.

Cherry Tabb Sharrer, Administrator/CEO
Minirth-Meier & Byrd Clinic, P.A.
Arlington, Virginia

Endnotes

Chapter 1 The Journey of Spiritual Discovery

1. B. Bettleheim, *Freud and Man's Soul* (Vintage, New York, 1984), 5.
2. N. C. Nielsen, Jr., *Solzhenitsyn's Religion* (Nashville: Thomas Nelson, 1975), 9.
3. Luke 8:10.
4. Proverbs 4:23.
5. John Bowlby, "Loss, Sadness, and Depression," *Attachment and Loss*, 3, monograph (London, 1980), 442.
6. C. S. Lewis, "Morality and Psychoanalysis," *The Best of C. S. Lewis* (Grand Rapids, Mich.: Baker, 1977), 473.
7. Gerald May, *Addictions and Grace* (San Francisco: Harper, 1988), 14.
8. *The Confessions of St. Augustine,* F. J. Sheed, trans. (New York: Sheed and Ward, 1942), 3.
9. Ephesians 1:18.
10. Victor Frankl, *Man's Search for Meaning,* in Stephen Covey, *The Seven Habits of Highly Effective People* (New York: Simon and Schuster, 1989), 69.

Chapter 2 Our Hurt Trail

1. 1 Corinthians 13:11.
2. Adapted from *Diagnostic and Statistical Manual of Mental Disorders,* 3rd ed., rev. (Washington, D.C.: American Psychiatric Association, 1987).

Chapter 3 Dealing with Our Inner Anger

1. John Bradshaw, *Healing the Shame the Binds* (Deerfield Beach, Fla.: Health Communications, 1988), 127.
2. Ephesians 4:32.
3. Ephesians 4:26–27.
4. Malcolm X, quoted in *The International Thesauraus of Quotations* (New York: Harper and Row, 1970), 9.

Chapter 4 Our Authority Card

1. Genesis 1:26.
2. Micah 6:8.

3. M. Scott Peck, *The Road Less Traveled* (New York: Simon and Schuster, 1978), 81.

Chapter 6   A Spirit of Grace: Love

1. John 13:1.
2. Romans 1:21.
3. *Diagnostic and Statistical Manual of Mental Disorders*, 3rd ed., rev.
4. S. M. Johnson, *Humanizing the Narcissistic Style* (London: Norton, 1987).
5. Gerald May, *Addiction and Grace*, (San Francisco: Harper, 1988).
6. Covey, *The Seven Habits of Highly Effective People*.
7. Dr. William Barclay, *The Gospel of Matthew* (Philadelphia: Westminister Press, n.d.), 338–39.
8. Ephesians 3:17–19.

Chapter 7   A Spirit of Oneness: Communion

1. Genesis 2:18.
2. Luke 22:15, 18.
3. Matthew 26:26–28.
4. A. Stassinopoulos, *Picasso* (New York: Simon and Schuster, 1988), 474.
5. Luke 18:1.
6. Thomas Keating, *Open Mind, Open Heart* (Rockport, Mass.: Element, 1991), 93.
7. Isaiah 30:15.
8. Romans 8:16, 26.
9. Philippians 4:6–7.
10. Psalm 86:11.
11. Henri Nouwen, *Reaching Out: The Three Movements of the Spiritual Life* (Image Books: New York, 1975).
12. Isaiah 26:3.
13. Ecclesiastes 4:9–10.

Chapter 8   A Spirit of Supernatural Power: Commitment Despite Resistance

1. John 13:2.
2. Ephesians 6:12.
3. 1 John 4:4.
4. 1 Samuel 15:24.
5. Romans 8:31.
6. Romans 8:35, 37–39.
7. Romans 8:28.

8. 2 Timothy 1:7.
9. Romans 8:32.

Chapter 9   A Spirit of Divestiture: Humility

1. Anne Morrow Lindberg, _Gift from the Sea_ (New York: Vintage Books, 1955), 33.
2. Ibid.
3. Matthew 18:3.
4. Pope John XXIII, _Journal of a Soul,_ Dorothy White, trans. (New York: McGraw-Hill, 1965), 278–79.
5. Augustine, quoted in Dan Wakefield, _Returning: A Spiritual Journey_ (Doubleday: New York, 1988), 245.
6. Lindberg, _Gifts from the Sea._
7. Thomas Kelly, _A Testament of Devotion_ ([qy: publishing info?].
8. Richard J. Foster, _Celebrations of Discipline_ (San Francisco: Harper and Row, 1978), 78–82.
9. Matthew 5:37.

Chapter 10   A Spirit of Inner and Outer Harmony: Simplicity

1. Lawrence Kohlberg, _Essays on Moral Development,_ vol. 1 (San Francisco: Harper and Row, 1987).
2. John 13:14–15.
3. Luke 10:29–37.
4. 1 Corinthians 13:3.
5. Matthew 26:17.
6. Matthew 26:18.
7. Billy Graham Evangelistic Association Newsletter, July 1992.
8. Matthew 25:40.
9. John 13:14–15, 17.
10. Psalm 27:1.
11. Peter Kreeft, _Making Sense Out of Suffering_ (Ann Arbor, Mich.: Servant Books, 1986), 64.
12. Albert Schweitzer, quoted in D. Wakefield, _Returning_ (New York: Doubleday, 1988), 227.
13. Matthew 22:37–40.
14. Francis A. Schaeffer, _The Great Evangelical Disaster_ (Westchester, Ill.: Crossway Books, 1984), 38–39.
15. Henry Wadsworth Longfellow, "A Psalm of Life," _Poetical Works of Longfellow,_ (London: Oxford University Press, 1965), 3.
16. Matthew 5:10–12.
17. Ephesians 5:25.

18. Longfellow, "A Psalm of Life."
19. Matthew 25:35.

Chapter 11 A Spirit of Blessing: Willingness to Serve and to Be Served

1. Richard J. Foster, *Celebration of Discipline* (San Francisco: Harper and Row, 1978), 110.
2. William Barclay, *The Gospel of John*, vol. 2 (Philadelphia: Westminster Press, 1975), 139.
3. Matthew 11:28–30.
4. 1 John 2:17.
5. James 4:14.
6. Ecclesiastes 12:8.
7. 2 Corinthians 4:18.
8. Luke 12:15.
9. James 2:1–4.
10. James 2:9.
11. 1 Peter 5:5–6.
12. Philippians 2:6–8.
13. Luke 18:9–14.
14. 1 Timothy 6:7.

Chapter 12 A Spirit of Eternity: A Transcendent Perspective

1. See John 13:5–8.
2. Matthew 26:8–13.
3. John 13:10.
4. Matthew 11:28.
5. Ephesians 5:26.
6. 1 John 1:9.
7. Galatians 6:2.
8. Paulo Freire, *The Pedagogy of the Oppressed* (New York: Seabury Press, 1973), 77.